A-LEVEL YEAR 2

STUDENT GUIDE

AQA

Economics

Individuals, firms, markets and market failure

Ray Powell and James Powell

Hodder Education, an Hachette UK company, Blenheim Court, George Street, Banbury, Oxfordshire OX16 5BH

Orders

Bookpoint Ltd, 130 Park Drive, Milton Park, Abingdon, Oxfordshire OX14 4SB

tel: 01235 827827

fax: 01235 400401

e-mail: education@bookpoint.co.uk

Lines are open 9.00 a.m.–5.00 p.m., Monday to Saturday, with a 24-hour message answering service. You can also order through the Hodder Education website: www.hoddereducation. co.uk

ISBN 978-1-4718-5676-1

First printed 2016

Impression number 5 4 3 2 1

Year 2020 2019 2018 2017 2016

This guide has been written specifically to support students preparing for the AQA A-level Economics examinations. The content has been neither approved nor endorsed by AQA and remains the sole responsibility of the authors.

Typeset by Integra Software Services Pvt. Ltd., Pondicherry, India

Cover photo: gui yong nian/Fotolia

Printed in Italy

Hachette UK's policy is to use papers that are natural, renewable and recyclable products and made from wood grown in sustainable forests. The logging and manufacturing processes are expected to conform to the environmental regulations of the country of origin.

Contents

Content Guidance

Questions & Answers

Multiple-choice questions

Data-response questions

Essay questions

Investigation question

■ Getting the most from this book

Exam tips

Advice on key points in the text to help you learn and recall content, avoid pitfalls, and polish your exam technique in order to boost your grade.

Knowledge check

Rapid-fire questions throughout the Content Guidance section to check your understanding.

Knowledge check answers

1 Turn to the back of the book for the Knowledge check answers.

Summaries

■ Each core topic is rounded off by a bullet-list summary for quick-check reference of what you need to know.

Exam-style questions

Commentary on the questions

Tips on what you need to do to gain full marks, indicated by the icon **e**

Sample student answers

Practise the questions, then look at the student answers that follow.

Commentary on sample student answers

Read the comments (preceded by the icon **e**) showing how many marks each answer would be awarded in the exam and exactly where marks are gained or lost.

Questions & Answers

[04] 'Decisions by firms to cooperate with each other are always against the public interest.'

Evaluate this statement and assess the view that cartels, such as the airline cartel mentioned in Extract C, should be investigated and policed solely by national competition authorities such as the UK Competition and Markets Authority, and not by the European Union competition authorities.   [25 marks]

e There are two parts to this question, but both are testing the skill of evaluation. The first part of your answer must consider the meaning of 'the public interest'. Your answer to the second part should be improved if you understand the meaning of the word 'subsidiarity'. This involves the delegation of cartel policy as much as possible to national governments.

Student answer

[01] There are 12 values in Extract A from which the median value is calculated. This means that with an even number of values, the middle two must be selected and then averaged. The middle two values are 32% and 34%, for which the average is 33%. The median market share of low-cost carrier passenger aircraft seats between 2002 and 2014 was thus 33%

e 2/2 marks awarded. A correct and fully explained calculation, which earns both marks. Even though in this case the explanation is not needed, it could still pick up a mark if there was a slip in the calculation.

[02] The data in Extract A suggest that the European airline market has become more competitive in recent years as low-cost airlines have taken a greater share of passenger seats from the traditional airline carriers. In 2003, the low-cost airlines accounted for only 16.5% of the total passenger seats, but in every year shown the low-cost airlines increased their share of the market. By the end of the period their share of seats had increased by 40.1%. This means that the low-cost airlines have taken a significant number of passengers from the traditional airlines in the 11-year period.

e 3/4 marks awarded. The answer shows a good understanding of the issue posed by the question but loses a mark for making a slight slip when stating the market share of the small airlines had increased by 40.1% rather than to 40.1%. Also, the answer does not state explicitly that the market power of large airlines has not increased, stating instead that the European airline market has become more competitive in recent years. It amounts to the same thing, but it is better to use the wording in the question.

[03] The European Commission defines a monopoly as any situation when a firm controls 25% or more of the market share in a given market. Air France has a dominant position in the domestic flights market in France because it has 80% of seat capacity', according to Extract B. Hence Air France can be described as having been able to behave like a monopoly because of the lack of competition in the market.

80   AQA Economics

■ About this book

The aim of this guide is to prepare students for the AQA A-level Paper 1 'Markets and market failure' examination and for the microeconomic parts of AQA A-level Paper 3. (The parts of the AQA A-level Paper 1 not covered in this guide are covered in Student Guide 1: *The operation of markets and market failure*. All the topics explained in this book could be examined in the A-level Paper 3, which is a synoptic paper testing the whole of the A-level specification.)

Content Guidance

The A-level specification sections 4.1.1 'Economic methodology and the economic problem' and 4.1.3 'Price determination in a competitive market' are not covered in this guide. For these you should read sections 3.1.1 and 3.1.2 of Student Guide 1. The Content Guidance section of this book therefore starts with the A-level specification section 4.1.2 'Individual economic decision making', before then covering specification sections 4.1.4 'Production, costs and revenue', 4.1.5 'Perfect competition, imperfectly competitive markets and monopoly', 4.1.6 'The labour market', 4.1.7 'The distribution of income and wealth: poverty and inequality' and finally 4.1.8 'The market mechanism, market failure and government intervention in markets'. You can read all the topics, one by one, before proceeding to the Questions & Answers section of the guide. Alternatively, you may decide to read a particular topic and then to read the corresponding part of the Questions & Answers section. With the exception of topics 4.1.1 and 4.1.3, which, as noted, are covered in Student Guide 1, this guide covers microeconomic topics in the order in which they appear in the AQA A-level 'Markets and market failure' specification.

Questions & Answers

You should read the Questions & Answers section of the guide either after reading all five specification topics in the Content Guidance section or bit by bit, having revised a selected topic on a particular part of the specification. This final section of the guide includes examples of all the forms of assessment in the A-level economics examination. These are multiple-choice questions (MCQs), data-response questions (DRQs), essay questions (EQs) and finally an extended investigation/case study question (IQ).

This guide should be used as a supplement to other resources, such as class notes, the AQA A-level Economics for A-level Year 2 textbook, the *Economic Review* magazine and *AS/A-Level Economics: My Revision Notes* (all published by Hodder Education). As this guide contains summaries rather than in-depth coverage of all the topics in the specification, you should not use the guide as your sole learning resource during the main part of the course. However, you may well decide to use the guide as the key resource in your revision programme. You are strongly advised to make full use of the Questions & Answers section, especially in the revision period when you should be concentrating on improving your examination skills.

Content Guidance

The AQA A-level specification for the 'Individuals, firms, markets and market failure' contains the following five sections: 4.1.1 'Economic methodology and the economic problem'; 4.1.2 'Individual economic decision making'; 4.1.3 'Price determination in a competitive market'; 4.1.4 'Production, costs and revenue'; 4.1.5 'Perfect competition, imperfectly competitive markets and monopoly'; 4.1.6 'The labour market'; 4.1.7 'The distribution of income and wealth: poverty and inequality'; and 4.1.8 'The market mechanism, market failure and government intervention in markets'. Two of these specification sections are not covered in this Student Guide, having been explained in full in Student Guide 1: *The operation of markets and market failure*. The two sections are 'Economic methodology and the economic problem' and 'Price determination in a competitive market', which are explained in full in sections 3.1.1 and 3.1.2 in Student Guide 1. Student Guide 1 also includes introductory coverage of production, costs and revenue (in section 3.1.3), of market structures (in section 3.1.4) and of the market mechanism, market failure and government intervention in markets (in section 3.1.5).

4.1.2 Individual economic decision making

Running through traditional or orthodox (neoclassical) economic theory is the assumption that economic agents such as individuals, households and the owners of firms always try to act in their self-interest, to maximise private benefit. For the owners of firms, this is to maximise profit, whereas for individual consumers and households, it is to maximise the utility, fulfilment of need, satisfaction or pleasure obtained from spending their limited incomes.

Behaviour consistent with achieving these objectives requires rational economic decision making and appropriate responses to the incentives provided by changing relative prices in the markets in which economic agents operate.

Imperfect information in the market place makes it difficult for economic agents to make rational decisions and is a potential source of market failure. Asymmetric information is illustrated by the fact that on many occasions, sellers possess more accurate information than buyers of the nature of the goods and services involved in the market transactions that are taking place.

The topic ends with a short survey of behavioural economics, which is a new part of the A-level specification. Behavioural economists question the assumption of traditional economic theory that individuals are rational decision-makers who endeavour to maximise their utility. Concepts such as choice architecture and framing, nudges, default choice and restricted choice are explained in the context of behavioural economics and economic policy.

4.1.4 Production, costs and revenue

This specification section covers knowledge of short-run and long-run production (including the law of diminishing returns and returns to scale), knowledge of how cost curves are derived from production theory in both the short run and the long run, and an understanding of economies of scale, diseconomies of scale and minimum efficient scale in relation to a firm's long-run average cost curve. The concepts of fixed cost and variable cost, and marginal cost, short-run average cost and total cost, must also be understood, along with total, average and marginal revenue. Student Guide 1 has already covered these topics – but without the marginal analysis required by the A-Level exam.

You must understand how technological change and technical progress affect the structure of markets and the production and consumption of goods and services, together with the impact of invention, innovation and technological change upon a firm's methods of production, its efficiency and its cost structure.

4.1.5 Perfect competition, imperfectly competitive markets and monopoly

This section of the A-level specification reintroduces you to the two extreme market structures of perfect competition and monopoly, both of which are examined in more depth in Student Guide 3 than in Student Guide 1. All the market structures that lie between the two extremes of perfect competition and pure monopoly are examples of imperfect competition. The two forms of imperfectly competitive market in this part of the specification are monopolistic competition and oligopoly, both of which are explained through the application of marginal analysis.

Covered in this topic are the distinctions between monopoly and monopoly power, and between different forms of competition such as price competition and non-price competition. The latter includes quality competition.

4.1.6 The labour market

This section of the specification requires application of supply and demand theory to the economy's labour markets.

In perfectly competitive labour markets, individual firms and workers are passive price-takers at the ruling market wage set in the market as a whole. By contrast, in monopsony labour markets, a single employer or buyer of labour has the market power to set the wage rate below the value of the marginal product of labour. Monopsony employers can also engage in wage discrimination, and discrimination according to gender, race or religion.

4.1.7 The distribution of income and wealth: poverty and inequality

Inequalities in the distribution of income and wealth and poverty are regarded by many economists as examples of market failure, a topic examined more broadly in the next and final topic of the Content Guidance section of this Student Guide.

Income and wealth, which are interlinked, provide examples of economic flows and stocks. Inequality of income and wealth often leads to poverty. Much of economists' focus on poverty is upon the difference between absolute and relative poverty.

AQA requires some knowledge of the distribution of household income and wealth in the UK. Students should understand that the degree of inequality can be measured but that whether or not a given distribution of income is equitable (fair and just) involves a value judgement. Students must be able to interpret Lorenz curves and Gini coefficients as measures of inequality, and to understand that excessive inequality is both a cause and a consequence of market failure.

4.1.8 The market mechanism, market failure and government intervention in markets

This section of the specification builds on the content of the similarly named section of the specification covered in Student Guide 1. The main difference between the coverage of the topic in Student Guides 1 and 3 lies in application of marginal analysis in Student Guide 3.

Markets may fail either because they perform inequitably (unfairly or unjustly) or because they perform inefficiently. Different people have different opinions about what is fair, so the first type of market failure depends on normative views or value judgements, explained in Student Guide 1. Many economists argue that inequalities in the distributions of income and wealth provide a significant example of market failure resulting from markets performing inequitably. Whenever markets are productively inefficient, or when they misallocate resources between competing uses, the second type of market failure occurs. Monopoly, explained earlier in the guide, is an important example. If the incentive function of prices breaks down completely, markets may be unable to produce any quantity of a good. Public goods provide an example, and there are also 'missing markets' in externalities. In other cases, markets may succeed in providing a good but end up providing the 'wrong' quantity. This happens if the market price is too high, which discourages consumption, or too low, which has the opposite effect of encouraging too much consumption. The main examples are merit and demerit goods.

When intervening in the market to maximise the public interest or social welfare, governments have various policy instruments at their disposal. The most extreme method of intervention involves abolishing the market, such as when the government provides public and merit goods directly and finances their provision through the tax system. At the other extreme, governments often allow markets to function largely free of intervention, but modified by the effect of taxes or minor regulation. Taxation and regulation provide the main forms of government intervention in markets. Other methods of intervention cited in the specification include subsidies, price controls and, in the case of negative externalities, permits to pollute.

Much government intervention attempts to correct the various market failures we have mentioned above. However, an attempt to correct market failure can lead to government failure. First, government intervention to correct a market failure or to achieve the government's objectives may simply be unsuccessful. Second, and often more seriously, completely new economic problems may emerge as a direct result of government intervention trying to correct other problems.

Individual economic decision making

These notes relate to AQA specification section 4.1.2 and prepare you to answer examination questions on:

- consumer behaviour
- imperfect information
- aspects of behavioural economic theory
- behavioural economics and economic policy.

Essential information

Consumer behaviour

Rational economic decision making and economic incentives

At the heart of traditional or orthodox demand theory is the assumption that the members of households or consumers always act rationally. Rational behaviour means people try to make decisions in their self-interest or to maximise their private benefit.

Given the assumption of rational economic behaviour, a change in the price of any good and a change in the conditions of demand (and/or supply), which leads to a change in price, alter the economic incentives facing a consumer.

With a traditional downward-sloping demand curve, a fall in the price of a good, relative to the prices of other goods, creates the incentive to demand more of the good. Likewise, an increase in the good's relative price creates an incentive to demand less of the good.

Utility theory: total and marginal utility

In economics, utility, which is the pleasure or satisfaction obtained from consumption, is usually divided into total utility and marginal utility. To explain the difference between total and marginal utility, let us imagine a thirsty child who drinks six glasses of lemonade on a hot sunny afternoon, deriving successively 8, 6, 4, 2, 0 and −2 'units of utility' from each glass consumed. This information is shown in Table 1 and plotted in Figure 1. Note that marginal utility is plotted at 'halfway' points.

Table 1 Total and marginal utility schedules for lemonade

Glasses of lemonade	Total utility (units of utility)	Marginal utility (units of utility)
0	0	
1	8	8
2	14	6
3	18	4
4	20	2
5	20	0
6	18	−2

Rational economic behaviour Acting in pursuit of self-interest, which for a consumer means attempting to maximise the welfare, satisfaction or utility gained from the goods and services consumed.

Utility The satisfaction or economic welfare an individual gains when consuming a good or service.

Marginal utility The additional satisfaction, welfare or pleasure gained from consuming one extra unit of a good or service.

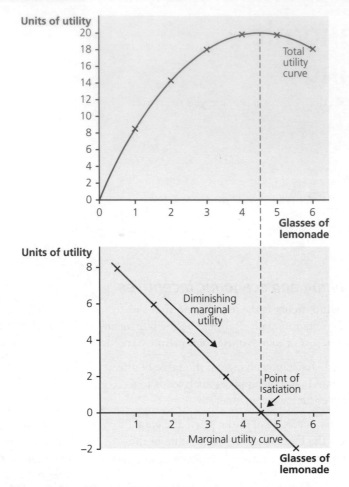

Figure 1 An example of total utility and marginal utility curves

The hypothesis or 'law' of diminishing marginal utility

The numerical examples in Table 1, and the graph in Figure 1, illustrate a very famous economic hypothesis, which some would call an economic law: the **hypothesis of diminishing marginal utility**. This simply states that as a person increases consumption of a good – while keeping consumption of other products constant – there is a decline in the marginal utility derived from consuming each additional unit of the good.

The assumption of maximising behaviour by economic agents (consumers, workers, firms and even the government) is central to orthodox or traditional economic theory. Economic agents decide their market plans so as to maximise a target objective or goal which is believed to be consistent with the pursuit of self-interest. In demand theory, the objective that households are assumed to wish to maximise is the utility, or satisfaction, obtained from the set of goods and services consumed.

Because of the problem of scarcity, consumers face a number of constraints which restrict the choices they make in the market place. The main constraints are limited time available, limited income and the given set of prices they face. Taken together, limited income and the set of prices faced impose a budget constraint on consumers'

Exam tip

The relationships between marginal values and total values of an economic variable must be understood when studying production theory, cost theory and revenue theory, as well as when studying utility theory. With production theory, cost theory and revenue theory, you must also understand the relationships between marginal and average returns, marginal and average cost, and marginal and average revenue.

Hypothesis of diminishing marginal utility For a single consumer the marginal utility derived from a good or service diminishes for each additional unit consumed.

Knowledge check 1

What is the difference between total utility and marginal utility?

freedom of action in the market place. As a general rule, a consumer can purchase more of one good only by giving up consumption of some other good or service, which represents the opportunity cost of consumption.

The importance of the margin when making choices

Along with assumptions such as rational economic behaviour and opportunity cost, the 'margin' is one of the key concepts in traditional or orthodox economic theory. Given consistent tastes and preferences, rational consumers choose between available goods and services in such a way as to try to maximise total utility, welfare or satisfaction derived from consumption of the goods. Along with the relative prices that must be paid for each of the goods, the marginal utilities gained from the consumption of the last unit of each good determine the combination of goods the consumer must choose in order to maximise total utility.

In order to maximise a desired objective, an economic agent must undertake the activity involved up to the point at which the marginal private benefit received equals the marginal private cost incurred. For example, a utility-maximising consumer must choose to consume or demand a good up to the point at which $MU = P$. Marginal utility, or MU, is the marginal private benefit derived from consuming the last unit of the good, while the good's price, P, is its opportunity cost in consumption, at the margin.

Imperfect information

The importance of information for decision making

When attempting to maximise total utility, more often than not consumers possess imperfect information. As a result, they make 'wrong' decisions. We saw in Student Guide 1 how consumers may choose to under-consume a merit good such as education and over-consume a demerit good such as tobacco because they possess imperfect information about the long-term consequences of their choices. We shall return to 'wrong' choices such as these later in this guide, and we shall also touch on this issue in our coverage of behavioural economics, which follows shortly.

The significance of asymmetric information

Asymmetric information arises when either the buyer or the seller involved in a potential transaction knows something that is not observable to the other party. One of the ways in which asymmetric information can manifest itself is through the process known as adverse selection, which is a feature of many market transactions. For example, in the sale and purchase of a second-hand computer, the seller of the good knows more about the computer's defects than a potential purchaser. However, to avoid paying too high a price for an inferior product which contains lots of defects, potential purchasers often offer low prices on all second-hand computers, regardless of the fact that some of the computers are good.

Aspects of behavioural economic theory

Behavioural economics has emerged in recent decades because of the dissatisfaction felt by some members of the economics profession with what they call traditional or orthodox economic theory. Traditional economic theories have been attacked by behavioural economists on the ground that the simplifying assumptions on which

---

Exam tip

The margin is one of the key concepts in A-level microeconomics. Make sure you understand and can apply the concept

Asymmetric information
When one party to a market transaction possesses less information relevant to the exchange than the other.

Knowledge check 2

Explain the difference between symmetric and asymmetric information.

Behavioural economics
A method of economic analysis that applies psychological insights into human behaviour to explain how individuals make choices and decisions.

the theories are built are unrealistic. In particular, in the context of what orthodox economists call the 'theory of the firm', which we begin to explain in the second topic, behavioural economists query the 'profit-maximising assumption'. This is the assumption that entrepreneurs make business decisions solely on the basis of whether the decisions will lead to larger profits. In the traditional theory of the firm, entrepreneurs are assumed to produce and sell output up to the point at which marginal revenue equals marginal cost, yet real-world business people seldom make such decisions when running their businesses.

We shall now look at some of the ways in which the approach of behavioural economists to economic problems and issues differs from that of traditional economics.

Bounded rationality

Traditional economists assume that, when exercising choice, individuals are perfectly rational, in the sense that they make decisions in a context of being fully informed, with perfect logic and aiming to achieve the maximum possible economic gain. However, in real life, individuals are seldom, if ever, perfectly rational. In the world in which we live, decisions are made in conditions of **bounded rationality**, which means that individuals, however high or low their intelligence, make decisions subject to three unavoidable constraints: imperfect information about possible alternatives and their consequences, limited mental processing ability, and a time constraint which limits the time available for making decisions. In complex choice situations, bounded rationality often results in *satisficing* rather than *maximising* choices.

Bounded self-control

Bounded rationality is closely linked to the related concept of **bounded self-control**. Traditional or orthodox economic theory implicitly assumes that when making choices, individuals have complete self-control. Behavioural economists, by contrast, believe that individuals have bounded (or limited) self-control. Making New Year resolutions in the period immediately after Christmas provides a good example. Having put on weight during the Christmas festivities, people may decide to go for a daily jog early in the morning before going to work each day after 1 January. For many, this may work well for a few days, but the first bout of bad weather often leads to the resolution being broken.

Biases in decision making

Behavioural economics argues that the decisions people make when exercising choice are often heavily biased. This is because decisions are made on the basis of one's likes, dislikes and experiences. Psychologists use the term **cognitive bias** to describe this situation.

A cognitive bias is a mental error that is consistent and predictable. There are many kinds of cognitive bias, one of which is confirmation bias. This is the tendency to seek only information that matches what one already believes. It stems from the often unconscious act of listening only to opinions that back up our pre-existing views, while at the same time ignoring or dismissing opinions – no matter how valid – that threaten our views.

Bounded rationality When making decisions, an individual's rationality is limited by the information they have, the limitations of their mind, and the finite amount of time available in which to make decisions.

Knowledge check 3

Give an example of irrational behaviour.

Bounded self-control Lack of the self-control needed to act to achieve perceived self-interest.

Cognitive bias A mistake in reasoning or in some other mental thought process occurring as a result of, for example, using rules of thumb or holding on to one's preferences and beliefs, regardless of contrary information.

Behavioural economists have identified a large number of cognitive biases that affect people's decision making. Biases in decision making often result from people following **rules of thumb**, which allow them to solve problems quickly. These rules of thumb enable people to function without always stopping to think about their next course of action. Even if people would like to make rational choices, they usually end up 'satisficing', accepting a satisfactory outcome rather than searching for an optimal solution. Bounded rationality often leads to people making rule-of-thumb decisions. Attempting to calculate and evaluate all possible outcomes often takes 'too much effort' and is too complicated.

Rule-of-thumb decisions are associated with what Daniel Kahneman has called 'System 1' or 'thinking fast', which is instinctive and emotional. Rules of thumb often serve us well, but they can also result in poor decisions which could have been improved if more 'effort' had been devoted to considering the alternatives available. Attempting to calculate and evaluate all possible outcomes often takes 'too much effort' and is too complicated. Kahneman's 'System 2', or 'thinking slow', is deliberate and logical but requires more effort and is often avoided, particularly for routine decisions.

Anchoring, which provides a good example of a bias in personal decision making, is the tendency to rely too much on a single piece of information, frequently the first piece of information, when making decisions. For example, the first price that is quoted for a product influences what people think is reasonable to pay for such a product. Charities, when seeking donations, may offer some suggestions, e.g. £20, £30 or £40, the purpose of which is to influence the decision making of a potential donor. Most people don't want to appear mean and might choose to donate £20, whereas without the anchor they might have given a smaller amount.

The **availability bias** relates to circumstances such as when people make judgements about the probability of events occurring in the future by how easy it is to recall examples of such events in the past. However, the recent occurrence of a particular event, and its consequences, is not necessarily a good guide to the underlying probability of such events occurring in the future. For example, after a period of severe flooding, people are likely to overestimate the likelihood of future floods and their costs. As a result, there may be a clamour to spend large amounts of money on flood defences that may not really be justified.

Human beings are social animals and as a result the behaviour of other people influences our own behaviour. By unconsciously learning from the behaviour of other people, **social norms** are established. Negative social norms include attitudes towards drinking alcohol. Many young adults often drink heavily because they think it is what people of their age are expected to do. By presenting statistical data showing that the majority of young adults do not engage in regular heavy drinking, behavioural economists would seek to nudge young adults into different patterns of behaviour.

Altruism is when we act to promote someone else's well-being, even though we may suffer as a consequence, either in terms of a financial or time loss or by incurring personal risk. Before the development of behavioural economics, economists generally assumed that individuals were not altruistic and acted only in their self-interest. Nevertheless, altruism could still be accommodated within maximising theory – for example, by assuming that individuals derive pleasure as a result of giving to others.

Rules of thumb Rough and practical methods or procedures that can be easily applied when making decisions.

Knowledge check 4

Explain how a striker in football makes decisions on how and when to shoot at goal in terms of 'thinking fast' and 'thinking slow'.

Anchoring A cognitive bias describing the human tendency when making decisions to rely too heavily on the first piece of information offered (the so-called 'anchor'). Individuals use an initial piece of information when making subsequent judgements.

Availability bias Occurs when individuals make judgements about the likelihood of future events according to how easy it is to recall examples of similar events.

Social norms Forms or patterns of behaviour considered acceptable by a society or group within that society.

Altruism Concern for the welfare of others.

More recently, behavioural economists have drawn attention to the fact that for many, if not most, people, their first impulse is to cooperate with each other rather than to compete. Very young children are frequently observed helping other children around them, out of a genuine concern for their welfare. Animals have also been observed displaying altruism.

Altruistic behaviour often results from people's perceptions of fairness. This being a normative term incorporating value judgements, different people have different views on the meaning of fairness. A popular view is that fairness involves treating people equally or in a way that is right or reasonable.

Behavioural economics and economic policy

In the context of the impact of behavioural economics on government economic policy making, you need to consider how behavioural economics might influence the design of a variety of government policies which aim to reduce or eliminate particular economic problems.

Behavioural economists do not deny that rational considerations play a part in people's decision making, but they believe that traditional economic models provide an incomplete account of the factors that influence the choices people make. Behavioural economic analysis extends the traditional model in an attempt to provide a better, more realistic explanation of human decision making.

The Behavioural Insights Team (BIT), set up by the Coalition Government in 2010, has suggested four ways in which behavioural insights can be applied to economic policy. These are to make it easy, attractive, social and timely for members of the general public to comply with the policy. In particular, the BIT focuses on default choices, which in turn relate to choice architecture. Choice architecture is the format in which choices are presented to the general public, for example to try to get individuals to make the choice which the policy maker is seeking.

Governments can use choice architecture in an attempt to achieve what they perceive to be a more socially desirable outcome. When making choices, people have a strong tendency to go with the default or pre-set option set out before them. Making the default the option the policy makers wish to be chosen makes it more likely that members of the general public will choose that option.

Individuals have a strong tendency to stick with the 'default' option, which is the outcome that occurs if they do not choose otherwise. A good example can be found with organ donation. If the default option is allowing organs to be donated in the event of the donor's death, more organs end up being donated than if people have instead to 'opt in' to give permission for their organs to be donated.

The use of nudges is an important part of the choice architecture. Nudges are used in government policy to change people's behaviour in a predictable manner without removing their freedom of choice. The use of nudges is an alternative to using laws to restrict or ban certain activities. Nudges attempt to influence people's decisions, and thereby increase social welfare, without the use of coercion. Since people are making decisions on the basis of incomplete information, without being nudged into desirable decisions, they are likely to make sub-optimal choices. The well-thought-out use of nudges can improve people's well-being.

Fairness The quality of being impartial, just, or free of favouritism. It can mean treating everyone the same. Fairness involves treating people equally, sharing with others, giving others respect and time, and not taking advantage of them.

Default choice An option that is selected automatically unless an alternative is chosen instead.

Choice architecture A framework setting out different ways in which choices can be presented to consumers, and the impact of that presentation on consumer decision making.

Nudges Factors that encourage people to think and act in particular ways. Nudges try to shift group and individual behaviour in ways that comply with desirable social norms.

Exam tip

Try to read Thaler and Sunstein's *Nudge: Improving Decisions about Health, Wealth and Happiness*, and also some of the Behavioural Insights Team's publications, which can be accessed on the internet.

People are influenced by how information is presented. Framing is the tendency for people to be influenced by the context in which the choice is presented when making a decision. Advertisers have for many years presented consumers with choices in a manner that frames their products in a favourable light. A statement on a cola bottle that its content is '95% sugar-free' works better for the manufacturer than a label stating 'contains 5% sugar'.

Framing How something is presented (the 'frame') influences the choices people make.

Examination skills

The skills most likely to be tested by data-response and essay questions on individual economic decision making at A-level are as follows:

- Knowledge of key demand concepts such as utility.
- Application of marginalist concepts such as marginal utility.
- Plotting of marginal and total utility curves from data in a question.
- Analysis of individual economic decision making in a market environment.
- Knowledge of differences between, but also occasional similarities of, traditional and behavioural economics.
- Awareness of the psychological foundations of behavioural economics.
- Knowledge of some of the key concepts and theories in behavioural economics.
- Evaluation of the extent to which behavioural economics can improve government economic policy.

Examination questions

In A-level Paper 1, a data-response or an essay question on a market may require knowledge of utility theory and/or knowledge of behavioural economics and the differences that separate traditional market theory and the approach of behavioural economists. Questions are likely to test the ability to use marginal analysis. In Section A of Paper 3, one of the 15 or so microeconomic MCQs is likely to be on behavioural economics, and a question on utility is also possible. MCQs 1, 2 and 3 in the Questions & Answers section of this guide provide examples of such questions. The first of the essay questions, on page 89 in the Questions & Answers section of this guide, is on behavioural economics. The approaches of behavioural economists may also be part of the scenario in the investigation question (IQ) in Section B of Paper 3: Economic principles and issues.

Common examination errors

Commonly made mistakes on individual economic decision making include the following:

- Lack of awareness of the different economic contexts in which individual economic decision making occurs: consumption decisions; supply of labour and other factor services; production decisions.
- Misunderstanding the role of maximising (and minimising) assumptions in traditional economic theory.
- Inability to apply marginal analysis to individual economic decision making.
- Failure to show understanding of the differences between, but also complementary aspects of, behavioural and traditional economics.

Summary

- The starting point for understanding individual economic decision making is understanding the nature of demand (explained in Student Guide 1), rationality and maximising behaviour.
- Economists have traditionally assumed that individuals wish to maximise utility, which can be thought of as satisfaction, pleasure or fulfilment of need.
- The hypothesis (or 'law') of diminishing marginal utility lies behind the derivation of an individual's demand curve.
- Individual economic decision making is affected by imperfect and asymmetric information.
- In recent years, behavioural economics has emerged to question many of the assumptions of traditional economic theory.
- Choice architecture and nudge theory lie at the heart of the ways in which behavioural architecture can influence economic policy making.

■ Production, costs and revenue

These notes relate to AQA specification section 4.1.4 and prepare you to answer examination questions on:

- the law of diminishing returns and returns to scale
- costs of production
- economies and diseconomies of scale
- marginal, average and total revenue
- profit
- technological change.

Essential information

Before reading about production, costs and revenue in this section, you should reread the similarly named section you will find on pages 23–26 of Student Guide 1: *The operation of markets and market failure*. The notes that follow build on the information initially explained in Student Guide 1. First, however, consider the content of Figure 2.

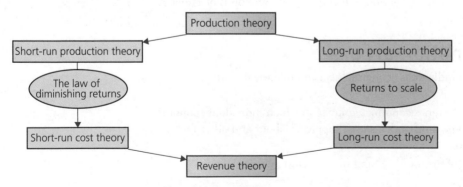

Figure 2 The three main 'building blocks' of the theory of the firm: production, costs and revenue

To understand the various market structures explained in the next topic in this Student Guide, it is first necessary to understand the nature of production, cost and revenue, depicted in Figure 2 as the 'building blocks' of the theory of the firm.

The law of diminishing returns and returns to scale
Developing short-run production theory

To remind you, in microeconomic theory, the short run is defined as the time period in which, in the course of production, at least one of the factors of production is fixed and cannot be varied. The only way in which a firm can increase output in the short run is by adding more variable factors of production such as labour to fixed factors of production such as capital.

The difference between marginal, average and total returns

Suppose a small manufacturing firm decides to employ only one worker. The worker must be a jack-of-all-trades, doing all tasks involved in production. But if more workers are hired, output can rise at a faster rate than the number of workers employed. This is because the workers benefit from specialisation and the division of labour, as production tasks are divided between the workers. In this situation, the marginal return of labour will increase. **Marginal return of labour** (marginal product) is the increase in output that results from adding an extra worker to the labour force. By contrast, the **average return of labour** is total output divided by the number of workers employed and the **total return of labour** is the total output of the labour force.

> **Marginal return of labour** The change in the quantity of total output resulting from the employment of one more worker, holding all the other factors of production fixed.

> **Average return of labour** Total output divided by the total number of workers employed.

> **Total return of labour** Total output produced by all the workers employed by a firm.

The law of diminishing returns

However, eventually, as more and more workers are combined with the firm's fixed capital, the benefits of further specialisation and division of labour come to an end. The **law of diminishing returns** (also known as the law of diminishing marginal productivity) sets in when the marginal product of labour starts to fall – that is, when one more worker adds less to total output than the previous worker who joined the labour force.

> **Law of diminishing returns** A short-term law which states that as a variable factor of production is added to a fixed factor of production, eventually both the marginal and average returns to the variable factor will begin to fall. It is also known as the law of diminishing marginal (and average) productivity.

Exam tip

Make sure you don't confuse the two words 'returns' and 'revenue'. One way of avoiding confusion is to prefer the term 'marginal product' to the term 'marginal return'.

Returns to scale

The law of diminishing returns is a short-run law that does not operate in the long run, when a firm can increase the scale of all its inputs or factors of production. You must not confuse the short-run law of diminishing returns with **returns to scale**, which occur only in the long run.

Exam tip

As we show shortly, the law of diminishing returns is important for explaining the shape of short-run cost curves, and likewise, returns to scale help to explain the shape of long-run cost curves and the concepts of economies and diseconomies of scale.

The difference between increasing, constant and decreasing returns to scale

With returns to scale there are three possibilities:

- **Increasing returns to scale.** An increase in the scale of all the factors of production causes a more than proportionate increase in output.
- **Decreasing returns to scale.** An increase in the scale of all the factors of production causes a less than proportionate increase in output.
- **Constant returns to scale.** An increase in the scale of all the factors of production causes an exactly proportionate increase in output.

Exam tip

Increasing returns to scale and economies of scale are often treated as interchangeable terms, though strictly speaking, returns to scale are part of long-run production theory whereas economies of scale are part of long-term cost theory. You must understand the relationship between returns to scale and economies or diseconomies of scale.

Costs of production

As well as confusing production with productivity, economics students often confuse production and **costs**. Production, as explained in Student Guide 1, simply converts inputs into outputs, without considering the money cost of using inputs such as capital and labour.

The difference between fixed and variable costs

As we have mentioned, in the short run, defined as the time period in which at least one factor of production is held fixed, costs of production divide into fixed and variable costs. Fixed costs are the costs a firm incurs when hiring or paying for the fixed factors of production. Capital is usually assumed to be a fixed factor of production. Variable costs, such as the costs of hiring many types of labour and buying raw materials, change as the firm's level of output changes.

Returns to scale The rate by which output changes if the scale of all the factors of production is changed.

Knowledge check 5

What is the difference between the law of diminishing marginal productivity and decreasing returns to scale?

Costs The money a firm has to pay out when hiring the services of the factors of production.

Knowledge check 6

Give two examples of fixed costs and two examples of variable costs.

At any level of output, a firm's total costs of production can be calculated by adding up the cost of producing each extra unit of output. Average costs, by contrast, are total cost divided by total output. Likewise, **average fixed cost** is total fixed cost divided by the level of output.

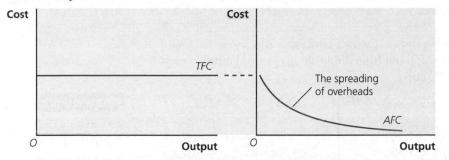

Figure 3 Total fixed cost and average fixed cost

Average fixed cost
Total cost of employing the fixed factors of production to produce a particular level of output, divided by the size of output: AFC = TFC ÷ output.

The left-hand panel of Figure 3 shows that total fixed cost (*TFC*) remains unchanged when output increases. Total fixed cost can be thought of as the cost of overheads, such as the rent a firm pays for leasing its buildings. However, the right-hand panel of the figure shows average fixed cost (*AFC*) per unit of output falling as output increases, since overheads are spread over a larger output.

The difference between marginal, average and total cost

Figure 4 shows an **average variable cost** (*AVC*) curve, with a **marginal cost** (*MC*) curve rising and cutting through the lowest point on the *AVC* curve. Marginal cost is the extra cost of producing one more unit of output. The shape of the *MC* curve is explained by marginal productivity theory. As long as the marginal productivity of labour is increasing, then, assuming all workers are paid the same wage rate, the cost of producing an extra unit of output falls. Hence marginal costs fall at low levels of output. But as soon as the law of diminishing returns sets in, an extra worker hired adds less to total output than the previous worker taken on. Total costs of production rise faster than output, leading to rising marginal costs.

Average variable cost Total cost of employing the variable factors of production to produce a particular level of output, divided by the size of output: *AVC* = *TVC* ÷ output.

Marginal cost Addition to total cost resulting from producing one additional unit of output.

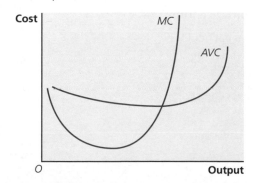

Figure 4 Average variable cost and marginal cost

The left-hand panel of Figure 5 shows how the firm's **average total cost** (*ATC*) curve is arrived at by adding up the *AFC* and *AVC* curves. The right-hand panel of Figure 5 shows the *ATC* curve without its two 'building blocks' (*AFC* and *AVC*). The *ATC* curve is U-shaped, showing that average total costs per unit of output first fall and later rise as output is increased. *ATC* must eventually rise because, at high levels of output, any further spreading of fixed costs is insufficient to offset the impact of diminishing returns upon variable costs of production. Eventually, rising marginal costs (which, as we have explained, result from diminishing marginal returns) must cut through and pull up the *ATC* curve.

> **Average total cost**
> Total cost of producing a particular level of output, divided by the size of output; often called average cost: $ATC = AFC + AVC$.

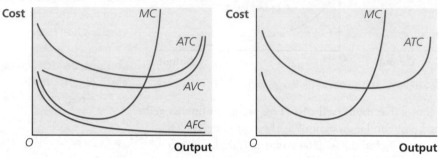

Figure 5 The average total cost curve results from adding *AVC* to *AFC*

The difference between short-run and long-run costs

So far, we have been explaining short-run costs of production, which are the costs incurred when at least one factor of production is held fixed. We now move on to explaining long-run costs of production. These are the costs incurred when all the factors of production are variable, in which case the scale or size of the firm can be changed.

Just as the short-run law of diminishing returns explains rising marginal costs and (eventually, when marginal costs cut through average total costs) rising average total costs, so we shall now use long-run production theory concepts to explain the firm's **long-run average cost** (*LRAC*) curve, illustrated in Figure 6. If, as the firm increases the size or scale of all its factors of production, it benefits from increasing returns to scale, the *LRAC* curve falls. Falling long-run average costs result when a firm benefits from an **economy of scale**. Conversely, a **diseconomy of scale** causes long-run average costs to rise. You should notice that a number of short-run average total cost (*SRATC*) curves, labelled $SRATC_1$, $SRATC_2$, $SRATC_3$ and $SRATC_4$, have been drawn in Figure 6, and that the *LRAC* curve touches (or is tangential to) each *SRATC* curve. Each *SRATC* curve represents a particular short-run size of firm.

> **Long-run average cost** Total cost of producing a particular level of output divided by the size of output when all the factors of production are variable.
>
> **Economy of scale** A cause of falling long-run average costs when a firm increases in size or scale.
>
> **Diseconomy of scale** A cause of rising long-run average costs when a firm increases in size or scale.

> **Knowledge check 7**
>
> Why are a firm's average variable cost (*AVC*) curve and its average total cost (*ATC*) curve U-shaped in the economic short run?

> **Knowledge check 8**
>
> How might an increase in wage rates, compared with the price of capital, affect a firm's costs of production and its demand for different factors of production?

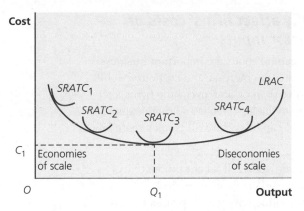

Figure 6 A long-run average cost curve

Figure 6 shows a U-shaped *LRAC* curve in which economies of scale and falling long-run average costs give way beyond $SRATC_3$ to diseconomies of scale. $SRATC_3$ represents the lowest unit cost and most **productively efficient size of firm**. This is also sometimes called the optimum size of firm. However, other shapes of *LRAC* curve are also possible.

> **Exam tip**
>
> Make sure you don't confuse the economic short run and the economic long run, and short-run cost curves and long-run cost curves.

> **Exam tip**
>
> Make sure you can illustrate economies and diseconomies of scale on a cost curve diagram.

Productively efficient size of firm The size or scale of firm which minimises long-run average costs.

The reasons for the shape of the marginal, average and total cost curves

Figures 4 and 5 illustrate the important relationship between any marginal curve and the average curve plotted from the same data:

- when the marginal > the average, the average rises
- when the marginal < the average, the average falls
- when the marginal = the average, the average is constant, neither rising nor falling.

The relationship between marginal and average curves has several economic applications: marginal and average product curves (in production theory); marginal and average cost curves (illustrated in Figures 5 and 6); and, as we shall explain shortly, marginal and average revenue curves. You must understand this relationship. It does not state that an average curve will rise when the related marginal curve is rising, or that the average curve must fall when the related marginal curve falls. Look again at Figure 5. After diminishing returns set in, the *MC* curve starts to rise, but the *AVC* curve continues to fall as long as marginal costs are below average variable costs. Eventually, however, the *MC* curve rises through the *AVC* curve, causing the *AVC* curve also to rise. As a result, the *AVC* curve is U-shaped, with the *MC* curve cutting through the curve at its lowest point.

At any level of output, total cost is the addition of the marginal costs of producing each successive unit of output. When marginal costs fall, the rate of increase of total cost slows down. But when marginal costs begin to rise, the rate of increase of total cost speeds up or accelerates.

How factor prices and productivity affect firms' costs of production and their choice of factor inputs

Factor prices such as wages and the price of capital goods are important business costs, of course. If they increase, costs of production increase and cost curves shift upward. And if labour becomes more expensive than capital, over time firms alter the nature of production, in the long run employing less labour and more capital. Conversely, if wages fall relative to the price of capital, firms will employ more labour and less capital.

To remind you, labour productivity is output per worker. If labour productivity increases, the real cost of labour falls, so more workers may be employed. Two points to note, however, are, first, increasing labour productivity mainly results from a firm employing more and better capital goods, and second, with increased labour productivity, fewer workers are needed to produce the same level of output.

Economies and diseconomies of scale

We mentioned the difference between economies of scale and diseconomies of scale in the earlier section on the difference between short-run and long-run costs, and illustrated the difference in Figure 6. To remind you, economies of scale are shown by falling long-run costs of production and diseconomies of scale by rising long-run costs of production.

Firms can benefit from various types or forms of economy of scale as they grow. These include technical economies of scale, managerial economies of scale, marketing economies of scale, financial or capital-raising economies of scale, risk-bearing economies of scale, and economies of scope.

The difference between internal and external economies of scale

The types of economy of scale listed above are all internal economies of scale, which result from the growth of the firm itself. By contrast, an **external economy of scale** results from the growth of the whole industry and market in which the firm exists. A similar distinction is made between an internal and an **external diseconomy of scale**.

Reasons for diseconomies of scale

Among the diseconomies of scale which firms suffer, and which raise long-run average production costs, are poor communication and coordination problems. With regard to the former, firms find it difficult to maintain an effective flow of information between the different parts of a large firm. With regard to the latter, large firms often find it much harder to coordinate different activities undertaken by a large labour force than a small firm does.

The relationship between returns to scale and economies or diseconomies of scale

To remind you, returns to scale are a part of long-run production theory. Economies and diseconomies of scale, by contrast, are a part of long-run cost theory. The two are related. For example, increasing returns to scale are a cause of technical economies of scale.

External economy of scale A fall in long-run average costs of production resulting from the growth of the market or industry of which the firm is a part.

External diseconomy of scale An increase in long-run average costs of production resulting from the growth of the market or industry of which the firm is a part.

The relationship between economies of scale, diseconomies of scale and the shape of the long-run average cost curve

Again to remind you, if you refer back to Figure 6, you will see that economies of scale are shown by falling long-run average costs, while diseconomies of scale are depicted by rising long-run average costs. Figure 6 shows the 'textbook' $LRAC$ curve, but other shapes are possible. One of these is shown in Figure 7.

The L-shaped long-run average cost curve

Figure 7 shows an L-shaped $LRAC$ curve. The size of firm represented by $SRATC_3$ is sited at the point on the $LRAC$ curve beyond which no more economies of scale are possible. But there are no diseconomies of scale, so all sizes of firms beyond this firm size are equally productively efficient.

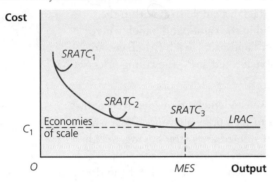

Figure 7 The 'L'-shaped $LRAC$ curve

The concept of the minimum efficient scale of production

The lowest point on the $LRAC$ curve shows the **minimum efficient scale** (MES) firm. As noted in the previous section, beyond this size of firm, no more economies of scale are possible. In Figure 7, the $LRAC$ curve is flat to the right of the MES size of firm. By contrast, with the U-shaped $LRAC$ curve shown in Figure 6, diseconomies of scale set in to the right of MES.

Marginal, average and total revenue

The difference between marginal, average and total revenue

Revenue is the money a firm receives from selling its output. **Marginal revenue** is the addition to **total revenue** received when an extra unit of output is sold. At any level of output, **average revenue** is total revenue divided by output, while total revenue is the addition of the marginal revenues received from each unit of output.

Why the average revenue curve is the firm's demand curve

To explain why its average revenue curve is the demand curve for a firm's output, we shall take the example of a perfectly competitive firm. (Perfect competition and other forms of market structure are explained in the next topic, starting on page 28.)

A perfectly competitive firm's revenue curves are derived from the assumptions that the firm can sell whatever quantity it wishes at the ruling market price, but that it cannot influence the ruling market price by its own action.

Minimum efficient scale Achieved after economies of scale have been benefited from to the full.

Marginal revenue Addition to total revenue resulting from the sale of one more unit of the product.

Total revenue Addition of the marginal revenues received from each unit of output.

Average revenue Total revenue divided by output.

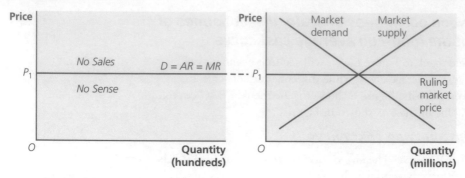

Figure 8 Deriving the *AR* and *MR* curves of a perfectly competitive firm

The right-hand panel of Figure 8 shows the whole of a perfectly competitive market, whereas the left-hand panel shows the situation facing a single firm within the market. The ruling market price P_1 is determined in the right-hand panel, where market demand equals market supply. In the left-hand panel, each firm faces an infinitely elastic or perfectly elastic demand curve located at P_1, the ruling price set by market forces in the whole market.

Consider also the two slogans, 'no sales' and 'no sense', which are respectively above and below P_1. Suppose, first, that the firm tries to set a price above P_1. Possessing perfect market information, the firm's customers immediately stop buying, deciding instead to buy the identical products (which are perfect substitutes) available at P_1 which are produced by other firms in the market – hence 'no sales'. But if the firm can sell as much as it wishes at the ruling price, there is no point in reducing the price below P_1. No extra sales are gained, but the firm loses sales revenue (and profit) – hence 'no sense'. We can conclude that a perfectly competitive firm is a **price-taker**, passively accepting, but unable to influence, the ruling market price.

As well as being the perfectly elastic demand curve for the firm's output, the horizontal line drawn through P_1 is the perfectly competitive firm's average revenue (*AR*) curve and its marginal revenue (*MR*) curve. Every time it sells one more unit of output, total sales revenue rises by the price at which the extra unit is sold (P_1). Thus marginal revenue is P_1. And because revenue per unit sold is always the same however much is sold, average revenue is P_1 at all levels of output and sales.

The relationship between average and marginal revenue

The relationship between average and marginal revenue is explained by the mathematical rule you read about on page 21. To remind you:
- when the marginal > the average, the average rises
- when the marginal < the average, the average falls
- when the marginal = the average, the average is constant, neither rising nor falling.

Figure 8 shows that in perfect competition, when $MR = AR$, the average is constant, neither rising nor falling. On page 32, we shall explain how, in monopoly, when $MR < AR$, the *AR* curve falls.

The relationship between marginal revenue and total revenue

Since total revenue is the sum of the marginal revenues received from each unit of sales, the total revenue curve rises at a constant rate in perfect competition

Price-taker A firm that is so small that it has to accept the ruling market price. If the firm raises its price, it loses all its sales; if it cuts its price, it gains no advantage.

Knowledge check 9

Distinguish between marginal revenue and marginal returns.

because *MR* is the same for each unit of sales. In monopoly, by contrast, *MR* falls as sales increase, with the result that the *TR* curve rises at a slower rate than output. Eventually, *MR* may become negative, in which case *TR* falls.

Profit

Students often confuse profit and revenue, mistakenly believing that the two terms have the same meaning. However, profit and revenue are different. **Profit** is the difference between the sales revenue a firm receives when selling the goods or services it produces and the costs of producing the goods.

> Total profit = total revenue − total costs

> **Exam tip**
>
> An exam question may ask you to plot cost and revenue curves from data presented in the question.

Profit The difference between sales revenue and costs of production.

Normal and abnormal profit

In the next topic on market structures, we shall see how economists distinguish between two theoretical profit concepts: **normal profit** and **abnormal profit**. Normal profit is the minimum level of profit necessary to keep existing firms in production, while being insufficient to attract new firms into the market. Because a firm must make normal profit to stay in production, economists treat normal profit as a cost of production, including it in a firm's average cost curve. In the long run, firms unable to make normal profit leave the market.

Abnormal profit, which is also known as supernormal profit and above-normal profit, is any extra profit over and above normal profit. In the long run and in the absence of entry barriers, abnormal profit performs the important economic function of attracting new firms into the market. However, in highly competitive markets, which in the real world means those that approximate to perfect competition, the entry of new firms into the market brings down the market price and whittles away abnormal profit, until in long-run or 'true' equilibrium, surviving firms make normal profit only.

Normal profit The minimum profit a firm must make to stay in business, which is, however, insufficient to attract new firms into the market.

Abnormal profit Profit over and above normal profit. Also known as supernormal profit and above-normal profit.

The role of profit in a market economy

Profit performs a number of roles in a market economy. These include the creation of business, worker and shareholder incentives. Profit also influences the allocation of resources, it is an efficiency indicator, and it is a reward for innovation and for risk taking. Finally, profits provide an important source of business finance.

Technological change

Technology is knowledge put to practical use to solve problems facing human societies. **Technological change**, by contrast, involves improving existing technologies and the development of completely new technologies, both to improve existing products and the processes involved in making the products, and to develop completely new products and processes.

Technological change A term used to describe the overall effect of invention, innovation and the diffusion or spread of technology in the economy.

The difference between invention and innovation

Invention refers to advancements in pure science, whereas innovation is the application of the new knowledge created by invention to production.

Through its diffusion into the economy, technological change affects methods of production, productivity, efficiency and firms' costs of production. With regards to methods of production, much recent technological progress has centred on mechanisation giving way to automation. And since this involves machines such as robots, rather than human beings, operating other machines, labour productivity (output per worker) obviously increases. The reorganisation of methods of production associated with automation causes average costs to fall, which leads to improvements in productive efficiency.

> Mechanisation Process of moving from a labour-intensive to a more capital-intensive method of production, employing more machines and fewer workers.

> Automation Automatic control where machines such as robots operate other machines.

The effects of technological change

In the economic sphere, technological change leads to the development of completely new markets, to changes in market structure, and also to the destruction of existing markets. It can affect methods of production, productivity, efficiency and firms' costs of production. Technological change can also influence the structure of markets. Technological change generally improves economic efficiency. By increasing productivity, over time technological changes shift downward both short-run and long-run cost curves. Firms create new products that satisfy people's needs and wants. Over time their actions improve social welfare.

Technological change is also part of a process known as creative destruction, in which economic growth occurs in the economy as a result of new innovations creating more economic value than that being destroyed by the decline of the technologies that the new innovations replace. Over time, societies that allow creative destruction to operate grow more productive and richer; their citizens benefit from new and better products and higher living standards.

Examination skills

The skills most likely to be tested by objective test or data-response questions on production, costs and revenue are as follows:
- Calculating costs, revenue and profit from given data.
- Plotting cost and revenue curves on a graph from given data.
- Relating cost, revenue and profit to a firm's assumed business objective, such as profit maximisation.
- Defining and explaining the meaning of production, specialisation, division of labour and economies and diseconomies of scale.
- Identifying different types of economy or diseconomy of scale.
- Relating specialisation and the division of labour to the role of markets in the economy.
- Relating over-specialisation and diseconomies of scale to the economic performance of a market.

> Invention Making something entirely new; something that did not exist before at all.

> Innovation Improves on or makes a significant contribution to something that has already been invented, thereby turning the results of invention into a product.

> Creative destruction The economy evolving and renewing itself over time through new technologies and innovations replacing older technologies and innovations.

Examination questions

In A-level Paper 1, a data-response or an essay question on production, costs and revenue is likely to test knowledge and understanding of marginal analysis. Such knowledge is likely to be linked to one or more of the various market structures which form the body of the next topic, covering perfect competition, imperfectly competitive markets and oligopoly. In Section A of Paper 3, two of the fifteen or so microeconomic MCQs are likely to be on production, costs and revenue, perhaps involving the interpretation of a graph. MCQs 4, 5 and 6 in the Questions & Answers section of this guide provide examples of such questions. The scenario in the investigation question (IQ) in Section B of Paper 3 may focus on the theory of the firm, in which production, costs and revenue is a significant sub-part.

Common examination errors

Commonly made mistakes on production, costs and revenue are:
- confusing short-run and long-run production and costs
- confusing returns and revenue
- incorrectly drawing and labelling cost and revenue curves and failing to plot them correctly from given data
- confusing economies and diseconomies of scale
- confusing internal and external economies of scale
- failing to appreciate the nature and role of technological change
- confusing innovation with invention.

Summary

- The building blocks of the theory of the firm include production theory, cost theory and revenue theory.
- Production and cost theory divide into short-run and long-run theory.
- The key concept in short-run production theory is the law of diminishing returns, also known as the law of diminishing marginal productivity.
- In the short run, the marginal cost curve and the average variable cost curve are derived from the law of diminishing marginal (and average) returns.
- Assuming that the variable factors of production experience diminishing returns, the average variable cost (AVC) and the short-run average total cost ($SRATC$) curves are U-shaped.
- The key concept in long-run production theory is returns to scale.

- The key concepts in long-run cost theory are economies and diseconomies of scale.
- The long-run average cost ($LRAC$) curve may be U-shaped, but other shapes are possible.
- Profit is total sales revenue minus total costs of production. Normal profit is just sufficient to keep incumbent firms in the market but is insufficient to attract new firms into the market.
- Abnormal, or supernormal, profit is any profit over and above normal profit.
- Diseconomies of scale are rising average costs of production when the size or scale of the firm increases.
- Technological change involves improving existing technologies and the development of completely new technologies, both to improve existing products and the processes involved in making the products, and to develop completely new products and processes.

■ Perfect competition, imperfectly competitive markets and monopoly

These notes relate to AQA specification section 4.1.5 and prepare you to answer examination questions on:

- market structures
- the objectives of firms
- perfect competition
- monopoly and monopoly power
- monopolistic competition
- oligopoly
- price discrimination
- the dynamics of competition and competitive market processes
- contestable and non-contestable markets
- market structure, static efficiency, dynamic efficiency and resource allocation
- consumer and producer surplus.

Essential information

Market structures

Whereas cost curves derive from production theory and the cost of hiring the factors of production, a firm's revenue curves depend on the market structure in which it sells its output. Figure 9 shows the main market structures recognised by economists.

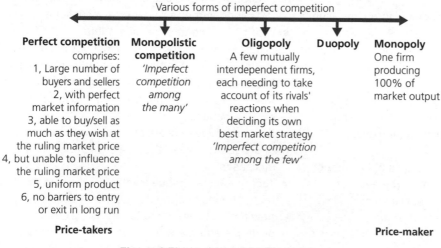

Figure 9 The main market structures

Perfect competition and **monopoly** are at opposite ends of the spectrum shown in Figure 9. In a perfectly competitive market there are a large number of firms. By contrast, in monopoly (or strictly, pure monopoly), a single firm produces the whole

Perfect competition
Best defined by the six conditions or characteristics of the market structure listed in Figure 9.

Monopoly A firm producing 100% of the market output.

of the output of a market or industry. A pure monopolist faces no competition at all, since there are no other firms to compete against. Monopolists do, however, usually face some competitive pressures, both from substitute products and sometimes also from outside firms trying to enter the market to destroy their monopoly position. Pure monopoly is exceedingly rare. Often the word 'monopoly' is used in a looser sense to refer to any highly concentrated market, in which one firm is dominant.

Every market structure between the extremes of perfect competition and monopoly illustrates a form of **imperfect competition**. There are two main forms of imperfect competition: **monopolistic competition** and **oligopoly**. Because there are a large number of firms in monopolistic competition, the market structure is often called 'imperfect competition among the many'. By contrast, an oligopoly is a market dominated by a few large interdependent firms. Interdependence means that an oligopolist has to take account of the likely reactions of the other firms when deciding price and output. The market structure is often called 'imperfect competition among the few'. **Duopoly** is a special case of oligopoly in which there are just two dominant firms.

Perfect competition is an abstract economic model that does not actually exist in any real-world market. This is because the conditions listed in Figure 9 which define perfect competition are too demanding and never occur together simultaneously. Competitive markets in the real world are examples of imperfect competition rather than perfect competition, though some highly competitive markets, such as commodity and financial markets, possess some of the features of perfect competition.

The objectives of firms

Economists usually assume that firms have a single business objective: to maximise profit. However, real-world firms may have other objectives, such as to maximise sales revenue, maximise the growth of the business or maximise managerial objectives. The last is significant when there is a divorce of ownership from control in a business, which occurs in large firms organised as public limited companies (plcs). Plcs are owned by thousands of shareholders who employ managers or executives to run the business. As business scandals in the early twenty-first century in firms such as Royal Bank of Scotland (RBS) have shown, the managers may pursue their own agendas, maximising their personal pay and making decisions that are not in the interests of the business's owners.

Firms may also be profit 'satisficers' rather than profit 'maximisers'. Under this assumption, decision-makers in firms, be they the owners of small corner shops or the chief executives of huge plcs, may be content with a satisfactory outcome, say satisfactory profit, rather than the best possible outcome. They may be happy with an easy life.

Perfect competition

Perfect competition short-run equilibrium

In the previous topic on production, costs and revenue, we explained how a perfectly competitive firm's revenue curves are derived from the assumptions that the firm can sell whatever quantity it wishes at the ruling market price, but that it cannot influence the ruling market price by its own action.

Imperfect competition A competitive market lying between the extremes of perfect competition and monopoly.

Monopolistic competition A market structure closer to perfect competition than to monopoly.

Oligopoly A market structure closer to monopoly than to perfect competition.

Duopoly Two firms only in a market.

Knowledge check 10

List three industries or markets that approximate to perfect competition (i.e. industries or markets that exhibit most but not all of the characteristics of perfect competition).

Figure 10 shows the equilibrium level of output produced by a perfectly competitive firm in the short run. The firm (shown in the left-hand panel of the diagram) has to accept the ruling price determined by market supply and demand (shown in the right-hand panel). As explained in the previous topic, the ruling price is also the firm's average revenue (AR) curve and its marginal revenue (MR) curve.

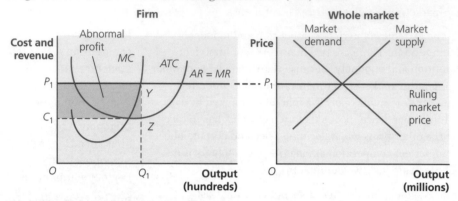

Figure 10 The short-run equilibrium level of output of a perfectly competitive firm

At this point in the analysis, we must introduce and explain the condition that must be met for a firm in *any* market structure – including perfect competition – to maximise profit. The firm must produce the level of output at which the marginal revenue it earns exactly equals the marginal cost incurred when producing this level of output: $MR = MC$. If the firm produces below this level of output (in which case $MR > MC$), then, by stepping up output, profit increases. Conversely, if the firm produces beyond the profit-maximising level of output (in which case $MR < MC$), then, by cutting back output, profit increases.

Using the $MR = MC$ condition, the firm's profit-maximising or equilibrium output is Q_1. At Q_1, total sales revenue (quantity sold times price) is shown by the area OP_1YQ_1. Likewise, total cost (quantity sold times average cost) is shown by the area OC_1ZQ_1. This means that the shaded area C_1P_1YZ shows abnormal profit (total revenue minus total cost). Abnormal profit can, of course, be made at levels of output other than Q_1 – indeed, at all levels of output at which price is above average cost. But at these levels of output profit is less than at Q_1. Only by producing and selling Q_1 can the firm make the largest possible abnormal profit.

Perfect competition long-run equilibrium

The short-run equilibrium shown in Figure 10 is a temporary equilibrium rather than a true equilibrium. In the short run, new firms cannot enter the market, so incumbent firms (i.e. firms already in the market) continue to make abnormal profit. However, in the long run, when there are no **entry** or **exit barriers** and firms can enter or leave the market freely, abnormal profit (shown by the shaded area in the left-hand panel of Figure 10) acts as a magnet, attracting new firms into the market. The entry of new firms shifts the market supply curve rightward from S_1 to S_2 in the right-hand panel in Figure 11. This causes the ruling market price to fall until it settles at P_2. Market and firm are now both in long-run or *true* equilibrium.

Entry barrier A barrier such as the protection provided by patent legislation that prevents new firms from entering and competing in a market.

Exit barrier A barrier, such as the large costs that would be involved, that prevents a firm from leaving a market.

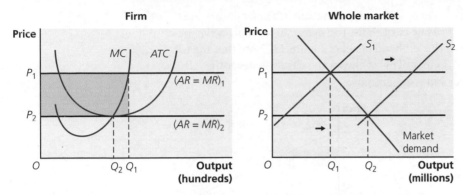

Figure 11 How long-run equilibrium is achieved in perfect competition

Figure 12 shows more clearly a perfectly competitive firm in long-run equilibrium. The price line just touches the lowest point of the firm's ATC curve, so no abnormal profit is made. Because the profit made by surviving firms is restricted to normal profit, the incentive for new firms to enter the market no longer exists.

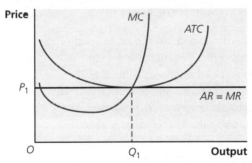

Figure 12 A perfectly competitive firm in long-run equilibrium

Monopoly and monopoly power

Before we explain how a monopoly maximises profit, we must first explain a monopolist's average revenue (AR) and marginal revenue (MR) curves. Monopoly revenue curves differ from those facing a firm in a perfectly competitive market. Because there is only one firm in the market, the **market demand curve** is the demand curve for the monopolist's output. This means that the monopolist faces a downward-sloping demand curve, which can affect the monopolist in one of two ways. If we regard the monopolist as a **price-maker**, then whenever it sets the price, the demand curve determines how much it can sell. If the monopolist tries to raise the price, it must accept a fall in sales. Alternatively, if the monopolist decides to act as a quantity setter, the demand curve dictates the maximum price at which any chosen quantity can be sold. Thus the downward-sloping demand curve means that the monopolist faces a trade-off. A monopoly cannot set price and quantity independently of each other.

Because the demand curve shows the price that the monopolist charges at each level of output, the demand curve is the monopolist's average revenue curve. Unlike perfect

Knowledge check 11

Why is it impossible to find real-world examples of perfect competition?

Market demand curve Shows how much of a good or service all the consumers in the market plan to demand at different possible prices.

Price-maker A monopoly possessing sufficient market power to choose the price at which it sells its output.

competition, however, marginal revenue and average revenue in monopoly are not the same. Because the average revenue curve falls, the marginal revenue curve must be below it. This is illustrated in the left-hand panel of Figure 13. Note that the MR curve is twice as steep as the AR curve. This is always the case whenever the AR curve is both downward sloping and a straight line.

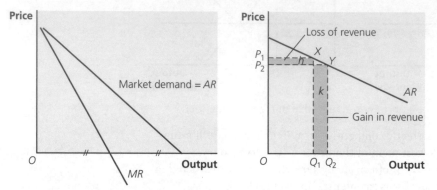

Figure 13 Monopoly average revenue and marginal revenue curves

The relationship between AR and MR in monopoly can also be explained in another way that is illustrated in the right-hand panel of Figure 13. Because the demand curve (AR curve) is downward sloping, the monopolist can sell an extra unit of output only by reducing the price (and average revenue) of all units of output sold. In this situation, total sales revenue *increases* by the shaded area k on the diagram, but *decreases* by the shaded area h. Area k shows a revenue gain, namely the extra unit sold multiplied by its price. By contrast, area h shows a revenue loss. The revenue loss results from the fact that, in order to sell one more unit of output, the price has to be reduced for *all* units of output, not just the extra unit sold. In monopoly, marginal revenue = the revenue gain *minus* the revenue loss, which must be less than price or average revenue.

Monopoly equilibrium

Just like a perfectly competitive firm, a monopoly maximises profit by producing the level of output at which $MR = MC$. In Figure 14, point A locates the profit-maximising level of output (Q_1). However, the price charged by the monopoly is located at point D on the demand curve (and AR curve), immediately above point A. Abnormal profit is shown by the shaded area C_1P_1DB. Unlike in perfect competition, the figure does not distinguish between short-run and long-run equilibrium. This is because in monopoly, entry barriers prevent new firms joining the market, thus enabling the monopoly to make abnormal profit in the long run as well as the short run.

In contrast to perfect competition, where abnormal profit is temporary, a monopoly makes abnormal profit as long as entry barriers protect it. Indeed, in monopoly, abnormal profit is often called monopoly profit, indicating the monopolist's power to preserve profit by preventing competition.

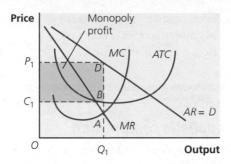

Figure 14 Monopoly equilibrium

Causes of monopoly and sources of monopoly power

Monopoly power stems from a firm's ability to exclude rivals from the market by imposing entry barriers. A pure monopoly obviously possesses monopoly power, but firms in imperfectly competitive markets such as oligopolies can also exercise monopoly power to a greater or lesser extent. Whereas perfect competition is characterised by consumer sovereignty (in the sense that firms respond to the wishes of consumers exercised through their pounds spent in the market), monopolies exercise and exploit producer sovereignty. Consumers cannot go elsewhere to buy the good, and are presented with a 'take it or leave it' choice. Enjoying producer sovereignty, a firm with monopoly power exploits consumers by restricting output and raising price, by limiting consumer choice, and by making permanent excess profit.

But even when a firm is a monopoly producer of a particular good or service, monopoly power is weak if close substitutes exist, produced by other firms in other industries. Monopoly power is greatest when the firm produces an essential good for which there are no substitutes. Factors that give rise to monopoly power include advantages of geographical location, control over raw material supply or market outlets, economies of scale, use of advertising, branding and product differentiation as entry barriers, and laws such as patent legislation, which protect innovations and intellectual property from copying.

Monopolistic competition

Monopolistic competition, which as we have mentioned is often called 'imperfect competition among the many', resembles perfect competition in the following ways:

- As in perfect competition, there are a large number of firms in the market.
- In the long run there are no barriers to entry or exit.
- As a result, the entry of new firms, attracted by short-run abnormal profits, brings down the price each firm can charge until only normal profits are made in the long run.

However, monopolistic competition resembles monopoly in two other ways:

- Each firm faces a downward-sloping demand curve. This results from the fact that each firm produces a slightly different product – differentiated by such features of modern production and marketing as style, design, packaging, branding and advertising. The goods produced by the various firms provide partial but not perfect

Knowledge check 12

What is the difference between monopoly and monopoly power?

Exam tip

Globalisation also has an important effect on monopoly power. Although a firm may appear to be a monopoly *within* a country, the firm's monopoly power will be considerably reduced if it has to compete with imports produced in other countries.

substitutes for each other. The resulting 'product differentiation' in the market means that each firm possesses a degree of monopoly power over its product. Unlike in perfect competition, if a firm raises its price, it does not lose all its customers because there is brand loyalty.

■ Each firm's marginal revenue (MR) curve is below its average revenue (AR) curve, which of course is the demand curve for the firm's output.

Short-run profit maximisation in monopolistic competition

Short-run profit maximisation in monopolistic competition is illustrated in Figure 15, which is very similar to profit maximisation in monopoly, illustrated earlier in Figure 14. However, in monopolistic competition the demand or average revenue curve represents demand for the goods produced by just one firm within the market rather than demand for the output of the whole market. And because the other firms within the market produce partial though not perfect substitutes, the demand curve facing the firm is likely to be rather more elastic at the prices each firm may decide to set than would be the case in pure monopoly.

The profit-maximising level of output, Q_1, is located below point A in Figure 15, where $MR = MC$, and the abnormal profits made by the firm in the short run are shown by the rectangular area $C_1 P_1 BD$.

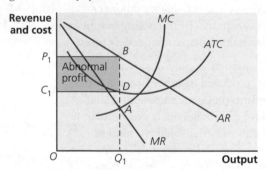

Figure 15 Short-run profit maximisation in monopolistic competition

Long-run profit maximisation in monopolistic competition

The absence of barriers to entry or exit in the long run is of great importance in the theory of monopolistic competition. Long-run profit maximisation in monopolistic competition is different in an important respect from profit maximisation in monopoly. In the long run, the entry of new firms causes the demand curve or AR curve facing an established firm to shift leftward or inward. The leftward shift may result from the introduction of new substitute products, attracting some customers away from the existing firms. Long-run profit maximisation is achieved when the AR curve forms a tangent to the firm's ATC curve, thereby removing the firm's abnormal profit.

This is shown in Figure 16, at point B immediately above level of output Q_1. Since only normal profit is made, total sales revenue and total costs of production are both shown by the rectangle $OP_1 BQ_1$. Note also that the point of tangency between the AR and ATC curves occurs immediately above point A, which determines the profit-maximising level of output Q_1 where $MR = MC$.

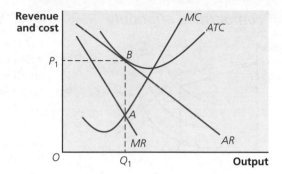

Figure 16 Long-run profit maximisation in monopolistic competition

Oligopoly

Oligopoly is a market structure in which a few large firms dominate the market. This means there is a high degree of market concentration, which can be measured by a **concentration ratio**. For example, a five-firm concentration ratio of 80% means that the five largest firms produce 80% of market output.

However, oligopoly is best defined by the behaviour or **conduct** of the firms within the market, rather than by market structure. Oligopolists are interdependent rather than independent, in the sense that they need to take account of the likely reactions of their rivals, the other oligopolists, when making price and output decisions. Consider, for example, an oligopolist who is thinking of raising the price charged in order to increase profit. Whether the price rise succeeds in increasing profit depends upon the likely reactions of the other firms. Will rival firms follow suit and match the price rise, or will they hold their prices steady, hoping to gain sales at the expense of the firm that raised the price? Clearly, when deciding whether to raise or lower its price, an oligopolist must make assumptions about the likely response of the other firms.

Competitive oligopoly

As noted, in competitive oligopoly a firm has to take account of the reactions of its rivals when forming its market strategy, but it does so without cooperating or colluding with the other firms. Uncertainty is a characteristic of competitive oligopoly – a firm can never be completely certain as to how rivals will react to its marketing strategy. Will they or will they not follow suit?

Collusive oligopoly

Uncertainty can be reduced by the rivals cooperating or colluding to fix prices or output, or even by allocating customers to particular members of the oligopoly. For example, by forming a **cartel** agreement or price ring, oligopolists can achieve a better outcome for them all, in terms of joint-profit maximisation and an easier life, than by remaining a competitive oligopoly. However, collusion or cooperative behaviour may not be good for the consumer, resulting in the disadvantages of monopoly, such as high prices and restriction of choice, without any of the benefits, such as economies of scale. For this reason, collusive oligopolistic arrangements such as cartel agreements are normally illegal, regarded by governments as against the public interest. In any case, it is seldom possible completely to eliminate uncertainty. Members of a cartel may cheat or renege on an agreement, secretly selling extra output at a price that undercuts the cartel's agreed price.

Oligopoly A market or industry in which there are a few dominant firms behaving interdependently.

Concentration ratio A measure of the total output produced in an industry by a given number of firms in the industry.

Knowledge check 13

What is the size of the industry concentration ratio for a pure monopoly?

Market conduct The way that firms behave in a particular market structure: for example, whether they compete, collude, set prices and levels of output, innovate or indulge in anti-competitive restrictive practices.

Cartel A group of colluding firms that fixes prices (forming a price ring) and perhaps also divides up the market by allocating maximum levels of output for each firm.

Knowledge check 14

Why may competitive oligopoly give rise to collusive oligopoly?

The kinked demand curve theory of competitive oligopoly

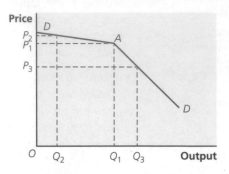 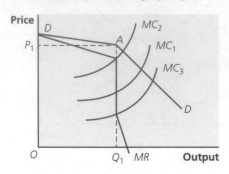

Figure 17 The kinked demand theory

The kinked demand curve theory, which is illustrated in Figure 17, can be used to explain a number of features of competitive oligopoly, such as interdependence, uncertainty and a preference for avoiding price wars. The theory was originally developed to explain price rigidity and the absence of price wars in oligopolistic markets. Suppose an oligopolist sells output Q_1 at price P_1 as shown in the left-hand panel of Figure 17. Because oligopolists lack accurate information about the demand and revenue curves they face, particularly at outputs other than those they are currently producing, each firm has to guess what will happen to demand if it changes its price.

The demand curve DD in Figure 17 represents an oligopolist's estimate of how demand will change with respect to either a price rise or a price fall. DD has been drawn on the assumption that the firm expects demand for its product to be relatively elastic in response to a price rise because rivals are expected to react by keeping their prices stable in the hope of gaining profits and market share. But the oligopolist expects demand to be relatively inelastic when the price is cut. This is because the oligopolist expects rivals to react to a price cut by decreasing their prices by the same amount. Few, if any, customers are likely to be lured away from rival firms.

The oligopolist therefore expects rival firms to react asymmetrically when price is raised compared with when price is lowered. The oligopolist's initial price and output, P_1 and Q_1, are located at the junction of two demand curves with different elasticities, each curve reflecting a different assumption about how rivals are expected to react to a change in price. The oligopolist expects profit to be lost whether price is raised or cut. On these assumptions, the best policy is to leave price unchanged.

Developing the kinked demand curve theory

The right-hand panel of Figure 17 illustrates a way in which the kinked demand curve theory can be developed further. As in all market structures, the demand curve facing an oligopolist is also its average revenue (AR) curve. But as we saw for monopoly, when AR falls, marginal revenue (MR) is below AR. You should note that the MR curve in the right-hand panel of Figure 17 has three sections. The uppermost section relates to the more elastic section of the AR curve to the left of the kink at point A, while the lowermost section relates to the less elastic section of the AR curve below and to the right of the kink. The mid-section of the MR curve is the vertical line joining the upper and lower sections of the MR curve below point A at the output level Q_1. Suppose the MC curve is initially MC_1. Since $MR = MC$ at this level of output, P_1 must be the profit-maximising price. However, if marginal cost rises or falls between MC_2 and MC_3, the profit-maximising output and price continue respectively to be Q_1 and P_1. The oligopolist's selling price remains stable despite quite significant changes in costs of production.

Weaknesses of the kinked demand theory

Although at first sight attractive as an explanation of price stability in conditions of oligopoly, the kinked demand theory has two significant weaknesses. First, it is an incomplete theory, since it does not explain how and why a firm chooses to be at point A in the first place. Second, evidence provided by the pricing decisions of real-world firms gives little support to the theory. Rival firms seldom respond to price changes in the manner assumed in the kinked demand curve theory, and it is also reasonable to expect that an oligopolist would test the market: that is, raise or lower the selling price to see whether rivals react in the manner expected. If the rivals did not, then the oligopolist would surely revise its estimate of demand for its product. Evidence conclusively shows that oligopoly prices tend to be stable or sticky when demand conditions change in a predictable or cyclical way, and that oligopolists usually raise or lower prices quickly and by significant amounts, both when production costs change substantially and when unexpected shifts in demand occur.

Non-price competition

The kinked demand curve theory suggests that oligopolists are reluctant to use **price competition** to gain sales and market share, although there is plenty of evidence that oligopolists do on occasion engage in **price wars**, even though, according to the kinked demand theory, such wars are self-defeating. Nevertheless, oligopolists also engage in many forms of **non-price competition**, such as marketing competition (for example, obtaining exclusive outlets such as tied public houses and petrol stations through which breweries and oil companies can sell their products), the use of persuasive advertising, product differentiation, brand imaging and packaging, and quality competition, including the provision of after-sales service.

Price discrimination

Oligopolists (and monopolists) sometimes use price discrimination to increase their profits. Price discrimination occurs when firms charge different prices to different customers based on differences in the customers' ability and willingness to pay. Those customers who are prepared to pay more are charged a higher price than those who are only willing to pay a lower price. It is important to understand that discriminatory prices are for the most part based on differences in demand conditions rather than on differences in costs of production. You should refer to the answer to the first part of Essay 2 in the Questions & Answers section of this guide for further explanation of price discrimination.

The dynamics of competition and competitive market processes

The traditional view in economics has been that price competition is the main form of competition in markets in which there are a large number of firms, but that markets become less competitive, at least in the form of price competition, as large firms become more dominant and market concentration increases.

Price competition Takes place when firms compete on the basis of low prices and value for money.

Price wars Occur when rival firms compete by reducing prices. A price cut by one firm provokes retaliation by its competitors.

Non-price competition Takes place when firms compete on the basis of quality, advertising, after-sales service and other non-price factors.

Knowledge check 16

Can all the differences in the prices charged by oligopolists be explained by the theory of price discrimination?

However, many economists now argue that all market structures in a capitalist economy can be highly competitive, although business decisions which on first sight may appear to be competitive are in fact 'anti-competitive' in the sense that they aim to increase the market power of already dominant firms. This view of competition is closely linked to the process of creative destruction, defined on page 26, an idea developed by the Austrian–American economist Joseph Schumpeter to explain the dynamic process through which capitalist economies change over time. Indeed, creative destruction has become the centrepiece for modern thinking on how economies evolve. Back in 1942, Schumpeter wrote: 'The opening up of new markets, foreign or domestic, incessantly revolutionises the economic structure from within, incessantly destroying the old one, incessantly creating a new one. This process of creative destruction is the essential fact about capitalism.'

Contestable and non-contestable markets

In **contestable market** theory, monopoly power is not dependent on the number of firms in the market or on concentration ratios, but rather on the ease or difficulty with which new firms may enter the market. Industrial concentration is not a problem, provided that an absence of barriers to entry and exit creates the ability for new firms to enter and contest the market. Actual competition in a market is not essential. According to this view, the threat of entry by new firms or potential competition is quite enough, according to contestable market theory, to ensure efficient and non-exploitative behaviour by existing firms within the market.

In recent years, contestable market theory has had a major impact upon UK monopoly policy. Instead of interfering with firms' pricing and output policies, governments should restrict the role of monopoly policy to discovering which industries and markets are potentially contestable. Deregulatory policies should be used to develop conditions in which barriers to entry and exit are minimised. In this way, non-contestable markets can be made contestable, though the existence of **sunk costs** may inhibit this process.

Market structure, static efficiency, dynamic efficiency and resource allocation

The specification requires you to be able to apply efficiency concepts when comparing the performance of firms in different market structures. In addition to understanding market structures, you must understand how **conduct indicators** and **performance indicators** can be used to compare market outcomes.

The left-hand and right-hand panels of Figure 18 respectively show a perfectly competitive firm and a monopoly in equilibrium – assuming that firms in both markets have similar ATC curves. This means there are no economies of scale. The figure shows that the perfectly competitive firm is productively efficient (producing where ATC is lowest), but that monopoly is productively inefficient (producing above minimum ATC). Likewise, the perfectly competitive firm is allocatively efficient (as $P = MC$), whereas the monopoly is allocatively inefficient (since $P > MC$). Compared with perfect competition, the monopoly's price is too high and its output is too low.

Contestable market A market in which the potential exists for new firms to enter the market. A perfectly contestable market has no entry or exit barriers and no sunk costs, and both incumbent firms and new entrants have access to the same level of technology.

Sunk costs Costs that have already been incurred and cannot be recovered.

Conduct indicators Information about a firm's conduct, e.g. its price-setting behaviour, which helps to indicate whether the firm's actions are competitive or anti-competitive.

Performance indicators Information about a firm's performance, e.g. its profit margins and investment record, which helps to indicate the extent to which the firm is protected from competition.

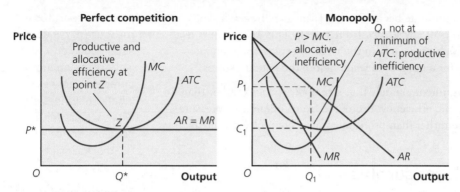

Figure 18 Evaluating perfect competition and monopoly in terms of economic efficiency

But is perfect competition necessarily more efficient than monopoly?

The conclusion made in the previous paragraphs that perfect competition is productively more efficient than monopoly depends partly on an assumption that there are no economies of scale. When substantial economies of scale are possible in an industry, monopoly may be productively more efficient than competition. Figure 19 illustrates a **natural monopoly** where, because of limited market size, there is no room in the market for more than one firm benefiting from full economies of scale. Producing on the short-run average cost curve $SRATC_N$, the monopoly may be producing above the lowest point on this particular cost curve, hence exhibiting a degree of productive inefficiency. However, all points drawn on $SRATC_N$ incur lower unit costs – and are productively more efficient – than any point on $SRATC_1$, which is the relevant cost curve for each firm were the monopoly to be broken up and transformed into a number of smaller competitive enterprises.

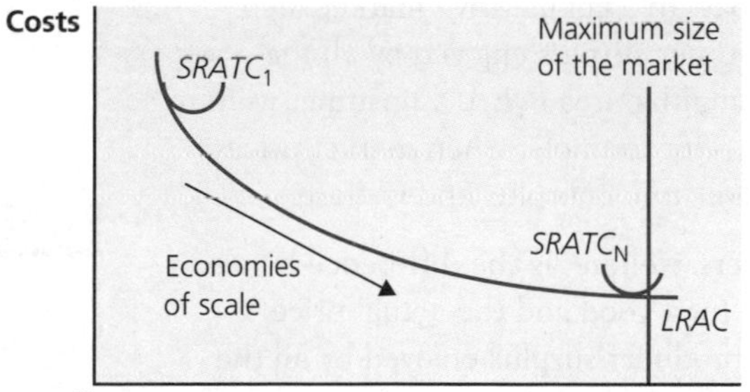

Natural monopoly
The term has two meanings: first, when a country or firm has complete control of a natural resource; second, when there is room in a market for only one firm benefiting to the full from economies of scale.

Figure 19 The justification of monopoly when economies of scale are possible

So far we have considered only **static efficiency** and not **dynamic efficiency**. As soon as we introduce dynamic efficiency into the analysis, monopolies can be justified on the ground that overall they may be more efficient than perfectly competitive firms. Protected by entry barriers, a monopoly can earn monopoly profit without facing the threat that the profit will be whittled away as new firms enter the market. This allows an innovating monopoly to enjoy the fruits of successful R & D and product development in the form of monopoly profit. In perfect competition, by contrast,

Static efficiency
Productive and allocative efficiency at a particular point in time.

Dynamic efficiency
Improvements in productive and allocative efficiency taking place over time.

there is little or no incentive to innovate because other firms can 'free-ride' and gain costless access to the results of any successful research. This argument is used to justify patent legislation, which grants a firm the right to exploit the monopoly position created by innovation for a number of years before the patent expires.

However, there is a counter-argument, namely that monopoly reduces rather than promotes innovation and dynamic efficiency. Protected from competitive pressures, a monopoly may profit satisfice rather than profit maximise, content with satisfactory profit and an easy life.

Consumer and producer surplus

To explain how market structures affect economic welfare, it is first necessary to introduce the concepts of **consumer surplus** and **producer surplus** as measures of welfare. Consumer surplus and producer surplus are illustrated in Figure 20.

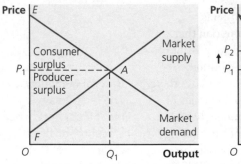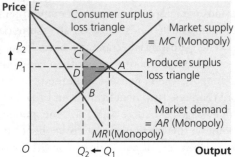

Figure 20 Market structure and economic welfare

Consumer surplus is the difference between the maximum price a consumer is prepared to pay and the actual price they need pay. In a competitive market such as the left-hand side of Figure 20, the total consumer surplus enjoyed by all the consumers in the market is measured by the triangular area P_1EA. Consumer welfare increases whenever consumer surplus increases – for example, when market prices fall. Conversely, however, higher prices reduce consumer surplus and welfare.

Producer surplus, which is a measure of producers' welfare, is the difference between the minimum price a firm is prepared to charge for a good and the actual price charged. In the left-hand side of Figure 20, the producer surplus enjoyed by all the firms in the market is measured by the triangular area FP_1A.

What may happen to economic welfare when monopoly replaces perfect competition?

The right-hand side of Figure 20 illustrates what can happen to economic welfare when monopoly replaces perfect competition (assuming there are no economies of scale). Market equilibrium in perfect competition is determined at point A: output is Q_1 and price is P_1. Monopoly equilibrium, by contrast, is determined at point B, where $MR = MC$. (Note that the marginal cost curve in monopoly is the same curve as market supply in perfect competition.) The figure illustrates the standard

Consumer surplus A measure of consumer satisfaction or welfare, being the difference between what consumers are willing to pay for a good or service and the market price they actually need pay.

Producer surplus A measure of producer welfare, being the difference between what producers are willing to accept in payment for a good or service and the market price they actually receive.

Knowledge check 17

What is meant by the term 'economic welfare'?

case against monopoly, namely that compared with perfect competition, monopoly restricts output (to Q_2) and raises price (to P_2). But we can now take the analysis one stage further and investigate how consumer surplus and producer surplus (and hence economic welfare) are affected. Raising the price from P_1 to P_2 transfers consumer surplus away from consumers and to the monopoly. The transfer is shown by the rectangle bounded by the points P_1P_2C and D. Producer surplus (in the form of monopoly profit) increases at the expense of consumer surplus. Over and above this transfer, there is also a net loss of economic welfare caused by the fact that the amount bought and sold falls to Q_2. The welfare loss (**deadweight loss**) is shown by the two shaded triangular areas in the right-hand panel of Figure 20. The upper triangle shows a loss of consumer surplus and the lower triangle shows a similar loss of producer surplus.

Examination skills

The skills most likely to be tested by objective test or data-response questions on perfect competition, imperfectly competitive markets and monopoly are as follows:

■ Identification of different market structures.
■ Applying knowledge and understanding of cost and revenue curves to perfect competition and monopoly.
■ Appreciating how price taking and price making affect analysis of perfect competition and monopoly.
■ Drawing and explaining a diagram to show a monopoly restricting output and raising the price.
■ Drawing and explaining a diagram to show a monopoly benefiting from economies of scale.
■ Evaluating market outcomes in different market structures.

Examination questions

In A-level Paper 1, a data-response or an essay question on perfect competition, imperfectly competitive markets and monopoly is likely to test your ability to analyse these market structures and to evaluate market outcomes using efficiency and welfare criteria. Data-response questions are likely to focus on real-world markets exhibiting features of oligopoly, monopolistic competition and/or monopoly. Because perfect competition is less likely to figure in a data-response question (for the simple reason that no real-world market is perfectly competitive), this market structure is more likely to appear in an essay question. However, because some real-world markets approximate to perfect competition, they could appear in any form of exam question. In Section A of Paper 3, about three of the fifteen or so microeconomic MCQs are likely to be on perfect competition, imperfectly competitive markets and monopoly, with a high likelihood of a graph featuring in such a question. MCQs 7, 8, 9 and 10 in the Questions & Answers section of this guide provide examples of such questions. DRQ 1 is on competition and monopoly in the European Union domestic airline market, while two of the three essay questions, Essay 2 and Essay 3, focus on market structure and related issues.

Deadweight loss The cost to society created by market inefficiency or the inefficient allocation of resources.

Knowledge check 18

How may monopoly lead to market failure?

Common examination errors

Commonly made mistakes on perfect competition, imperfectly competitive markets and monopoly are:

- failing to apply correctly the $MR = MC$ rule, particularly for monopoly equilibrium
- confusing short-run and long-run equilibrium in perfect competition
- failing to understand the difference between monopoly and monopolistic competition
- defining oligopoly solely in terms of market structure rather than the firms' interdependence
- failing to understand the theory of price discrimination
- confusing the different types of economic efficiency
- failing to appreciate the economies of scale and dynamic efficiency justifications of monopoly

Summary

- Perfect competition and monopoly are the extreme forms of market structure separated by imperfect competition.
- In the short run, perfectly competitive firms can make abnormal profit, but in the long run, market forces eliminate abnormal profit.
- True equilibrium in perfect competition occurs when surviving firms make normal profit only.
- Because a monopoly is protected by barriers to market entry, it can make abnormal profit (monopoly profit) in the long run.
- Monopolistic competition must not be confused with monopoly.
- Oligopoly is a market structure dominated by a few firms.
- In terms of market conduct or behaviour, the extent to which a market is oligopolistic can be judged by the extent to which the firms are interdependent.
- Price discrimination involves charging prices on the basis of how much consumers are prepared to pay.

- A high degree of interdependence leads to uncertainty about how rival oligopolists will react to a firm's market strategy, which in turn creates an incentive to collude and to form cartels.
- The theory of the kinked demand curve can be used to model oligopoly behaviour.
- If there is no scope for economies of scale, in the long run perfect competition is productively and allocatively efficient; by contrast, monopoly is productively and allocatively inefficient.
- In the long run, by contrast, economies of scale may result in monopoly being more productively efficient than perfect competition. Likewise, a monopoly may be more dynamically efficient.
- In terms of economic welfare, when monopoly replaces perfectly competition, the monopoly gains at the expense of consumers (i.e. consumer surplus is replaced by producer surplus).

■ The labour market

These notes relate to AQA specification section 4.1.6 and prepare you to answer examination questions on:

- the demand for labour, marginal productivity theory
- influences upon the supply of labour to different markets
- the determination of relative wage rates and levels of employment in perfectly competitive labour markets
- the determination of relative wage rates and levels of employment in imperfectly competitive labour markets
- the influence of trade unions in determining wages and levels of employment
- the national minimum wage
- discrimination in the labour market.

Essential information

Labour market theory is really just the price theory that you have studied in the goods market of the economy, but operating in the factor market, which is the market for the services of factors of production. Households and firms function simultaneously in both markets, but their roles are reversed. In the labour market, which is part of the factor market, firms demand labour services that households supply. As with the goods markets, which we looked at in Student Guide 1, we shall start by explaining the demand for labour, then switch to the supply of labour, before bringing demand and supply together in the context of a perfectly competitive labour market.

The demand for labour, marginal productivity theory

Firms demand labour because they believe profit can be made by selling the goods produced by their workers. This means that the demand for labour is a **derived demand**. Just as the market supply curve of labour in a perfectly competitive labour market is the sum of the supply curves of the individual workers in the labour market, so the market demand curve for labour is the sum of the demand curves for labour of each firm in the market.

Marginal revenue product and marginal physical product

Each firm's demand curve is the **marginal revenue product** (*MRP*) of labour curve facing the firm in the labour market. The marginal revenue product curve shown in panel (c) of Figure 21 is obtained by multiplying the **marginal physical product** (*MPP*) of labour, shown in panel (a), by marginal revenue (*MR*), shown in panel (b). The *MPP* of labour is just another name for the marginal returns (marginal product) of labour, which you first came across in the second topic in this guide, production, costs and revenue, on page 17. Because of the law of diminishing returns, the marginal product of labour falls as additional workers are hired. As its name indicates, the *MPP* curve shows only the physical output produced by an extra worker – measured in whatever goods the firm produces. To convert this into a money value, the *MPP* of labour must be multiplied by marginal revenue. The end result is the *MRP* curve:

marginal physical product × marginal revenue = marginal revenue product

Derived demand Demand for a good or service derived from the fact that the good or service is needed in the production of another good or service. An increase in the demand for the latter causes the demand for the input to increase.

Knowledge check 19

Test your synoptic knowledge by explaining the difference between derived demand and composite demand.

Marginal revenue product The monetary value of the addition to a firm's total output brought about by employing one more worker.

Marginal physical product The addition to a firm's total output brought about by employing one more worker.

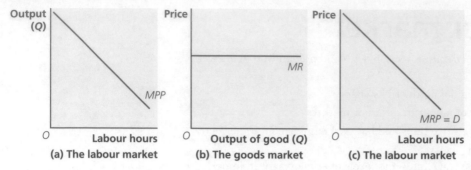

Figure 21 Deriving a firm's demand curve for labour (the *MRP* curve) from the *MPP* curve

Influences upon the supply of labour to different markets

The market supply curve of labour is obtained by adding together the individual supply curves of all the workers in the market. A worker's decision to supply one more hour of labour time must also mean that they sacrifice an hour of leisure time. For the worker to supply more labour, the hourly wage rate must rise to compensate for the fact that, as more money is earned, an extra pound means less and less, but an extra hour of leisure time sacrificed means more and more. (In economic terminology, the marginal utility of money falls and the marginal utility of leisure time rises as the worker supplies more labour, which eats into leisure time.)

The resulting upward-sloping supply curve of labour is shown in Figure 22(a). At the going hourly wage rate, a worker will not wish to supply labour beyond the point at which marginal utility of the wage = the marginal utility of leisure, other things remaining equal. At this point, the wage received from the last hour worked yields the same utility as the last hour of leisure time enjoyed. To make it worthwhile for a worker to supply labour beyond this point, the hourly wage rate must rise – for example, from W_1 to W_2 in Figure 22(a). It is possible, however, that the supply curve may bend backward above a certain wage rate (W_2 in Figure 22(b)), showing that as the wage rate rises above a critical level, the worker chooses to work fewer hours.

> **Exam tip**
>
> This is another application of the concept of marginal utility, which is explained in the first topic in this guide: individual economic decision making.

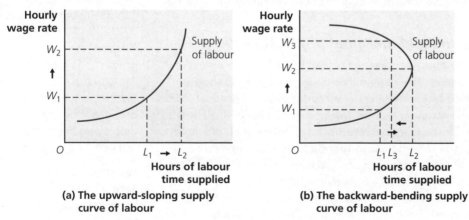

Figure 22 An individual worker's supply of labour

The supply of labour to different labour markets will also be affected by the **elasticity of supply of labour**. Factors that determine the wage elasticity of supply of labour include the following:

- The supply of unskilled labour is usually more elastic than the supply of a particular type of skilled labour. This is because the training period of unskilled labour is usually very short, and any innate abilities required are unlikely to be restricted to a small proportion of the total population.
- Factors that reduce the occupational and geographical mobility of labour tend to reduce the elasticity of labour supply.
- The supply of labour is also likely to be more elastic in the long run than in the short run.
- The availability of a pool of unemployed labour increases the elasticity of supply of labour, while full employment has the opposite effect.

The determination of relative wage rates and levels of employment in perfectly competitive labour markets

A perfectly competitive labour market, if it were to exist, would have to meet all of the following conditions at the same time. As would be the case in a perfectly competitive goods market, a perfectly competitive labour market would have to contain a large number of buyers and sellers, each unable to influence the ruling market price (in this case, the ruling market wage), and operating in conditions of perfect market information. Employers and workers would be free to enter the labour market in the long run, but an individual employer or firm could not influence the ruling market wage through its independent action.

Just as in a perfectly competitive goods market, it is impossible for all these requirements to be met simultaneously. It follows that perfectly competitive labour markets do not exist in the real world. Some labour markets, such as the market for building labourers in a city or region in which there is a very large number of small building companies, approximate to perfect competition, but nevertheless they are not perfectly competitive.

However, assuming perfect competition does exist, we are now in a position to show the determination of the equilibrium wage rate and level of employment, both for a single firm or employer within the market and for the whole of the labour market. These are shown respectively in panel (a) and panel (b) of Figure 23. The equilibrium wage rate W^* and level of employment L^* are determined in panel (b), where market demand equals market supply. Panel (a) then shows each firm as a price-taker at wage rate W^*, which, as well as being the perfectly elastic supply curve of labour facing each firm, is the **average cost of labour** (AC_L) curve and the **marginal cost of labour** (MC_L) curve. Because a firm can hire as many workers as it wants at W^*, every time an extra worker is hired, the firm's total wage bill rises by the wage paid to the new worker. Thus MC_L equals the ruling wage, which is also the AC_L (wage cost per worker).

Elasticity of supply of labour Proportionate change in the supply of labour following a change in the wage rate.

Average cost of labour Total wage costs divided by the number of workers employed.

Marginal cost of labour Addition to a firm's total cost of production resulting from employing one more worker.

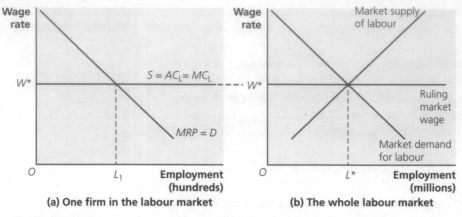

Figure 23 The equilibrium wage rate and level of employment in a perfectly competitive labour market

Knowledge check 20

Explain why firms and workers in a perfectly competitive labour market are passive price-takers.

To maximise profit when eventually selling the output produced by labour, the firm must demand labour up to the point at which:

- the addition to sales revenue from employing an extra worker = the addition to production costs from employing an extra worker

or:

- $MRP = MC_L$

In a perfectly competitive labour market, MC_L always equals the ruling wage, so the firm hires labour up to the point at which the marginal revenue product of labour equals the wage rate ($MRP = W$). This is L_1 in Figure 23(a).

> **Exam tip**
>
> It is important to remember that perfect competition does not occur in the real world – either in goods markets for products or in labour markets. Perfect competition should be regarded as a theoretical abstraction against which real-world markets can be judged, particularly in relation to competitiveness, efficiency and economic welfare.

The determination of relative wage rates and levels of employment in imperfectly competitive labour markets

A labour market in which there is a single employer is called a **monopsony**, and a market dominated by a single employer, but in which there are some other employers, is monopsonistic.

A monopsony is similar to a monopoly in many ways. As in monopoly, where consumers cannot choose between alternative suppliers of the good, in a monopsony labour market, workers cannot choose between alternative employers: only one firm or employer is available to hire their services. And in the same way that the market demand curve facing a monopoly supplier of a good is also the monopolist's average revenue curve, so the market supply curve of labour is the monopsonist's average cost of labour (AC_L) curve.

Monopsony One buyer only in a market.

Knowledge check 21

Explain why a monopsony employer is a price-maker rather than a passive price-taker.

The AC_L curve shows the different wage rates that the monopsonist must pay to attract labour forces of different sizes. For example, Figure 24(a) shows a monopsonyemployer hiring ten workers at a daily wage or AC_L of £100 each. The figure shows that with ten workers initially employed, the wage (or AC_L) must rise from £100 to £110 a day to attract an eleventh worker.

But in a monopsony labour market, the AC_L curve is not the marginal cost of labour (MC_L) curve. To attract extra workers, the monopsonist must raise the daily wage rate, paying the higher rate (in the absence of **wage discrimination**, which we shall explain shortly) to all its workers. In this situation, the MC_L incurred by employing an extra worker includes the total amount by which the wage bill rises and not just the wage paid to the additional worker hired. The MC_L curve is thus above the AC_L or supply curve (whereas in a goods market, a monopolist's MR curve is below its AR curve). In Figure 24(a), the MC_L of employing the eleventh worker is £210 a day. This comprises the £110 paid to the eleventh worker (the green area in Figure 24(a)), plus the £10 extra now paid to each of the original ten workers, which totals £100 (shown by the orange shaded area in Figure 24(a)).

Wage discrimination
Paying different workers different wage rates for doing the same job.

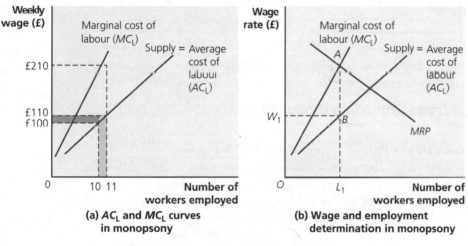

(a) AC_L and MC_L curves in monopsony

(b) Wage and employment determination in monopsony

Figure 24 A monopsony labour market

Figure 24(b) shows the equilibrium wage and level of employment in a monopsony labour market. As in a perfectly competitive labour market, the firm's equilibrium level of employment is determined where $MRP = MC_L$. This is at point A in Figure 24(b). However, the equilibrium wage is below A and thus less than the MRP of labour, being determined at point B on the supply curve of labour. Although the monopsonist could pay a wage determined at A and equal to the MRP of labour, without incurring a loss on the last worker employed, it has no need to. The monopsonist can employ all the workers required by paying the wage W_1, determined at point B.

Exam tip

Exam questions on monopsony are usually quite difficult and the standard of students' answers is often quite low. Think carefully before you choose to answer a question on a monopsony labour market.

The influence of trade unions in determining wages and levels of employment

A trade union is an association of workers formed to protect and promote the interests of its members. A union's main function is to bargain with employers to improve wages and other conditions of work. Acting as a monopoly supplier of labour, a union may try to set the wage rate above the market-clearing wage rate, leaving employment to be determined by the amount of labour that employers hire at the wage set by the union.

The effect of forming a trade union in a perfectly competitive labour market

Figure 25 shows the effect of a union setting the wage rate above the market-clearing rate in a (previously) perfectly competitive labour market. Employment falls from L_1 to L_2.

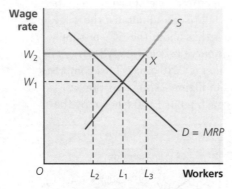

Figure 25 The effect of introducing a trade union into a previously perfectly competitive labour market

The effect of forming a trade union in a monopsony labour market

In the monopsony labour market shown in Figure 26, a union may be able to raise both the wage rate and employment. In the absence of a union, the employment level is L_1, determined at point A where $MRP = MC_L$, and the wage rate is W_1, determined at point B. If the union sets the wage rate at W_2, the kinked line W_2XS becomes the labour supply curve (and also the AC_L curve) facing the monopsonist employer. However, at wage rate W_2, the monopsonist's MC_L curve is the 'double-kinked' line W_2XZV. Employment rises to L_2, the level of employment at which the MRP curve intersects the vertical section between X and Z at point C on the double-kinked MC_L curve. Both the wage rate and employment have risen compared with the situation without a union.

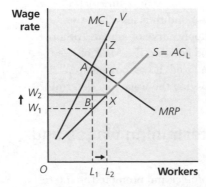

Figure 26 The effect of introducing a trade union into a monopsony labour market

The national minimum wage

Figure 26 can also be used to explain and analyse the possible effects of introducing a **national minimum wage (NMW)** rate. In a competitive labour market, a minimum wage rate set at W_2 increases wages for the workers who keep their jobs, but creates unemployment. By contrast, both wages and employment may rise if the labour market is monopsonistic. In 2016, the UK government began the process of replacing the NMW with a national living wage.

Discrimination in the labour market

Just as price discrimination occurs when firms with monopoly power charge different prices based on customers' different willingness to pay, so wage discrimination takes place when employers with monopsony power pay different wage rates based on workers' different willingness to supply labour. In the absence of wage discrimination, all workers in a competitive labour market (shown in Figure 27) receive a wage rate of W_1, determined by supply and demand. Employers' total wage costs are shown by the rectangle bounded by points OW_1AL_1. But if, instead of paying W_1 to all workers, employers pay each worker the minimum they are prepared to work for, the total wage bill falls to equal the shaded 'wedge' area bounded by the points $OBAL_1$. Employers thus gain at the expense of workers, which is why firms pay, and trade unions resist, discriminatory wages whenever possible.

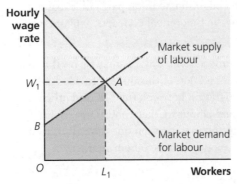

Figure 27 Wage discrimination

Other explanations of different wages

Even in highly competitive labour markets, wage differences exist, largely because the labour demand and supply curves are in different positions in different labour markets, reflecting factors such as varying labour productivity, ability and required skill. Also, different jobs have different non-monetary characteristics, often in the form of job satisfaction or dissatisfaction. Other things being equal, a worker must be paid a higher wage to compensate for any relative unpleasantness in the job. An equalising wage differential is the payment that must be made to compensate a worker for the different non-monetary characteristics of jobs so that, following the payment, the worker has no incentive to switch between jobs or labour markets.

Different wages paid to different groups of workers may also result from forms of labour market discrimination unrelated to the theory of wage discrimination. Some employers discriminate on the basis of race, religion, gender and age, even though such discrimination is usually illegal. Workers suffering labour market discrimination

National minimum wage (NMW) Hourly wage rate set by the government, which is an example of a price floor. It is illegal to pay a wage rate below the NMW.

Exam tip

Exactly the same theories, namely perfect competition theory and monopsony theory, should be used to analyse the effects of introducing a trade union or a national minimum wage into a labour market.

Knowledge check 22

Distinguish between the national minimum wage and the national living wage.

have poorer job opportunities and are generally less well paid than workers fortunate enough to avoid such discrimination.

Examination skills

The skills most likely to be tested by examination questions on the labour market are as follows:

- Understanding of role reversal between firms and workers in labour markets.
- Analysis of the determination of wage rates and levels of employment in different labour markets.
- Application of production theory learned when studying production and cost theory to firms' demand for labour.
- Understanding the reasons for different wage rates in different occupations.
- Appreciation of the similarities of, and the differences separating, monopoly and monopsony theory.
- Analysis of the effect of trade unions in different labour markets.

Examination questions

Essay questions in the examination are likely to ask for explanation, analysis and evaluation of the functioning of different labour markets (perfectly competitive and/ or monopsonistic), whereas data-response questions might home in on particular real-world labour markets and require the application of the theoretical concepts explained in these notes to the issues posed by the question.

In Section A of Paper 3, one of the fifteen or so microeconomic MCQs may be on the labour market. MCQ 13 in the Questions & Answers section of this guide provides an example of such a question. DRQ 2 on labour migration between the UK and other EU countries centres on how different wage rates and labour market conditions affect the international mobility of labour. The scenario in the investigation question (IQ) in Section B of Paper 3 may focus on a competitive or monopsonistic labour market.

Common examination errors

Commonly made mistakes on the labour market are:

- failing to understand the reversal of roles of households and firms in the labour market, with firms exercising demand for labour and households exercising supply
- failing to appreciate that maximising principles (profit for firms and utility for workers) underlie labour market theory
- writing about the whole market when the question asks for analysis of one firm within the market, and vice versa
- inaccurate analysis of the demand for labour in terms of marginal productivity theory
- lack of understanding of monopsonistic labour markets
- writing 'common-sense' superficial accounts of wage differences without using labour market theory.

Summary

- In labour markets, workers supply labour and firms or employers demand the services of labour.
- In a perfectly competitive labour market, the MRP curve is an employer's demand curve for labour.
- In perfect competition, the market supply of labour is the sum of the supply curves of labour of all the workers in the labour market.
- Likewise, in perfect competition, the market demand for labour is the sum of the demand curves of labour of all the employers in the labour market.
- In perfect competition, the equilibrium wage is set where market demand equals market supply, and all the firms and workers in the market are passive price-takers at the market-set wage.
- To maximise profit in all labour markets, firms employs workers up to the point at which $MRP = MC_L$.

- However, the wage rate and level of employment are lower in monopsony than for the whole of a perfectly competitive labour market.
- If a trade union is formed in a previously perfectly competitive labour market, any wage rate increase it achieves is likely to reduce the demand for labour.
- However, in monopsony, a trade union may, within certain limits, be able to increase both the wage rate and the level of employment.
- Similar outcomes result if a national minimum wage is imposed in perfectly competitive and monopsony labour markets.
- Wage discrimination takes place when employers with monopsony power pay different wage rates based on workers' different willingness to supply labour.

■ The distribution of income and wealth: poverty and inequality

These notes relate to AQA specification section 4.1.7 and prepare you to answer examination questions on:

- the distribution of income and wealth
- the problem of poverty
- government policies to alleviate poverty and to influence the distribution of income and wealth.

Essential information

The distribution of income and wealth

The difference between income and wealth

Income and wealth illustrate the key difference between flow and stock concepts in economics. Income is a flow, measured per period of time – for example, weekly, monthly or annually. The stock of wealth, by contrast, accumulates over time. The different factors of production receive different types of income. Employees are paid wages and salaries; owners of land and property receive rent; interest is paid to lenders of financial capital; and profit is the residual earned by the owners of businesses and entrepreneurs. Transfers, such as unemployment benefits, are another very important type of income, especially for the poor. As the name indicates, transfers shift income

Income A continuing flow of payments received on a regular basis.

Wealth The current value of assets accumulated over time.

Flow and stock concepts A stock is measured at one specific time while a flow is measured over a period of time, for example monthly, quarterly and annually.

from taxpayers to benefit recipients, without production of a good or service by the person receiving the benefit.

Various factors which influence the distribution of income and wealth

In the UK, as in most other countries, the distributions of income and wealth are both unequal, but the distribution of wealth is significantly more unequal than the distribution of income. The link between wealth and income partly explains this. For the better-off, wealth generates investment income, part of which – being saved – then adds to wealth and generates even more income. The poor, by contrast, who possess little or no wealth, also have incomes (from low-paid jobs and/or welfare benefits) that are too low to allow saving and the accumulation of wealth. The tax system also provides an explanation. In the UK, income is usually taxed, but wealth is generally untaxed, though when it is taxed, the rich can often avoid paying wealth taxes.

The distribution of income measures how personal or household income is distributed among different income groups in society, such as between rich and poor. Among the factors that influence the distribution of income are employment and unemployment, sickness and disability, possession or lack of possession of qualifications and skills, age, and whether or not one lives in a country or region of high employment and pay. Taking the working population as a whole, employed workers enjoy higher incomes than the unemployed, whose only source of income is welfare benefits set below average levels of wages and salaries. For a similar reason, people dependent on sickness and disability benefits generally suffer from low incomes. High incomes are also strongly correlated with qualifications and skills, and workers living in areas of high employment and job opportunity enjoy higher incomes than those living in areas of deprivation. While some of the elderly living beyond retirement age enjoy comfortable private pensions, the same is not true for older people solely dependent on the state pension, which is regarded by many as a poverty income.

People can hold wealth in physical assets such as land, houses, art and antiques, or in financial assets such as stocks and shares. Houses and shares are forms of **marketable wealth**, whose value can appreciate (go up in value) or depreciate (go down in value). Some forms of wealth are non-marketable. An example of **non-marketable wealth** is the stock of wealth accumulated when a person contributes to a pension scheme which cannot be sold to someone else.

Wealth can be divided into inherited wealth, which is passed on from one generation to the next, and non-inherited wealth, which is often the result of entrepreneurial flair and skill. These are sometimes called 'old wealth' and 'new wealth', though on or before their death the creators of 'new wealth' often decide to pass it on the next generations in their families. For both the owners of 'new' and 'old' wealth, the ability to save generated by the high incomes that wealth yields leads to the accumulation of even more wealth in future years.

The difference between equality and equity in relation to the distribution of income and wealth

Complete **equality of income** is achieved when each person receives exactly the same amount of income. The degree of inequality is indicated by the extent to which people's incomes differ. Equality (and inequality) are thus positive concepts,

Knowledge check 23
Why is income a flow and wealth a stock?

Marketable wealth
Assets such as houses and stocks and shares which can be sold.

Non-marketable wealth
Assets such as a claim on a future pension which cannot be sold.

Equality of income
Everybody, or all households, receiving the same income.

which can be measured. By contrast, **equity**, which means fairness or justness, is a normative concept, which cannot be measured. Different people form different value judgements on what is equitable or inequitable.

Horizontal equity involves treating people in the same circumstances equally, in contrast to vertical equity, which involves taking income from the rich on the grounds that they do not need it and redistributing this income to the poor on the grounds that they do need it.

The Lorenz curve and Gini coefficient

The extent to which the distribution of income is equal or unequal can be illustrated on **Lorenz curve** diagrams, such as that drawn in Figure 29, with the degree of inequality measured by a statistic known as a **Gini coefficient**.

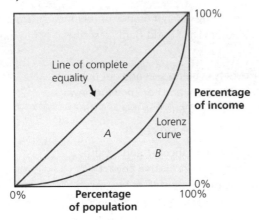

Figure 28 The Lorenz curve

> **Equity** Relates to whether people are treated fairly.

> **Lorenz curve** A line drawn on a graph which shows the extent to which income is equally or unequally distributed among the population.

> **Gini coefficient** Measure of income inequality based on the Lorenz curve.

The Lorenz curve in Figure 28 shows population on the horizontal axis, measured in cumulative percentages from 0% to 100%. The vertical axis shows the cumulative percentage of income received by the population. If incomes were distributed equally, the Lorenz curve would lie along the diagonal line. The nearer the Lorenz curve is to the diagonal, the more equal is the distribution of income. The Gini coefficient measures the area between the Lorenz curve and the diagonal as a ratio of the total area under the diagonal.

In terms of the figure, the Gini coefficient is calculated using the following formula:

$$\text{Gini coefficient} = \frac{\text{area } A}{\text{area } A + \text{area } B}$$

The lower the value of the Gini coefficient, the more equally household income is distributed.

The likely benefits and costs of more equal and more unequal distributions

It is sometimes argued, particularly by economists who favour government intervention in markets, that a more equitable or fair distribution of income and wealth can lead to faster economic growth. People on low incomes and who possess little wealth generally spend all or most of their incomes on consumption and save very little, or nothing at all. Greater spending on consumer goods and services increases aggregate demand in the economy, which promotes economic growth. By contrast, the better-off spend a smaller fraction of their incomes on consumption, which leads to slower growth.

Inequality can also mean that the talents of some people in society are wasted or, at least, not fully exploited. For example, children from families on low incomes are likely to do less well than children with affluent parents. Inequality in income usually means that there is also inequality of opportunity.

However, economists of a more pro-free-market persuasion generally reject this view of the world, partly on the ground that it takes no account of incentives and disincentives. They argue that the progressive taxation of higher incomes and wealth, combined with the transfer of taxed income to the less well off, in the form of welfare benefits, significantly reduces the incentives to work hard, both among the better-off and among the poor.

The problem of poverty

Poverty is the state of being extremely poor and not having enough money or income to meet basic needs, including food, clothing and shelter. The World Bank describes poverty in the following way:

> Poverty is hunger. Poverty is lack of shelter. Poverty is being sick and not being able to see a doctor. Poverty is not having access to school and not knowing how to read. Poverty is not having a job, is fear for the future, living one day at a time.

The difference between relative and absolute poverty

Poverty is closely related to inequalities in the distribution of income and wealth. However, we must distinguish between **absolute poverty** and **relative poverty**. Because the UK is a high-income developed economy, in which welfare benefits provide a minimum income and safety net for most of the poor, very few people are absolutely poor. For the most part, the problem of poverty in the UK is one of relative poverty. A household is in relative poverty if its income is below a specified proportion of average income for all households – for example, less than a third of average income. Possible causes of relative poverty include unemployment, especially long-term unemployment, old age and longevity, single parenthood, the decline of employment opportunities in traditional industries and skill fields, lack of education and training, the fall in the value of welfare and unemployment benefits relative to wages and salaries, and the higher incomes and tax cuts enjoyed by the better-off.

By contrast, absolute poverty occurs when income is below a particular specified level. When all incomes grow, absolute poverty falls, but relative poverty falls only if low incomes grow at a faster rate than average incomes.

The causes and effects of poverty

Three of the main causes of relative poverty in the UK are old age, unemployment and the low wages of many of those in work. Old age causes relative poverty largely because many old people rely on the state pension and lack a private pension. Unemployment benefits are generally lower than the pay workers received before losing their jobs. An increase in unemployment therefore increases poverty. In terms of low wages, the low-waged poor are almost always relatively poor rather than absolutely poor. In contrast, some of the unwaged, including homeless people living on the street, fall into the category of the absolutely poor.

In terms of its effects, poverty leads to educational deprivation, health deprivation and adverse effects on the communities in which the poor live. Children from poorer backgrounds lag at all stages of education. In terms of health deprivation, poverty is

Poverty The state of being poor.

Absolute poverty Not having the amount of income needed to meet the minimum requirements for one or more basic living needs over a period of time.

Relative poverty When people lack the minimum amount of income needed in order to maintain the average standard of living in the society in which they live.

also associated with a higher risk of both illness and premature death. Poorer health over the course of a lifetime has an impact on life expectancy: professionals live, on average, 8 years longer than unskilled workers. And finally, with regard to the effect of poverty on communities, children living in poverty are likely to live in bad housing.

Old-age poverty and the fact that the old are living for longer lead to other adverse effects on society, for example elderly but poor 'bed-blockers' continuing to occupy hospital wards after they have been successfully treated, simply because they have nowhere else to go.

Government policies to alleviate poverty and to influence the distribution of income and wealth

By reducing inequalities in the distribution of income, progressive taxation and transfers (welfare benefits) can reduce absolute and relative poverty – providing labour market incentives, competitiveness and economic growth do not worsen significantly. Absolute poverty, though not necessarily relative poverty, can best be reduced by fast and sustained economic growth and by creating jobs. It follows that successful government policies that promote economic growth alleviate poverty and influence the distribution of income and wealth.

When describing and explaining the distribution of income, it is useful to understand the difference between a number of measures of income: original income, gross income, disposable income, post-tax income and final income. The relationship between these different measures of income is shown in Figure 29.

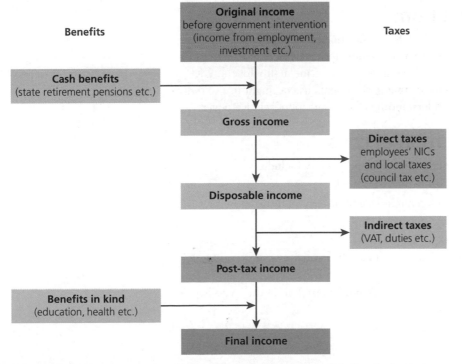

Figure 29 The different ways in which income is measured and their relation to taxes and benefits

Exam tip

Exam questions may frequently be set on absolute and relative poverty. Make sure you don't confuse the *causes* of poverty with the economic *effects* of poverty, and with government policies to reduce poverty, particularly progressive taxation and transfers.

Knowledge check 24

Distinguish between progressive, regressive and proportionate taxation.

The tax and welfare benefits systems affect income in the following ways. First, household members begin with income from employment, private pensions, investments such as the shares they own, and other non-government sources. This is referred to as 'original income'. Second, some then receive income from cash benefits. The sum of cash benefits and original income is referred to as 'gross income'. They then pay direct taxes. Income after direct taxes have been subtracted from gross income and cash benefits are added is called 'disposable income'. Indirect taxes are then paid on spending on goods and services. Disposable income minus indirect taxes is referred to as 'post-tax income'. Finally, many households receive a benefit from services provided by the government (benefits in kind). Post-tax income plus benefits in kind is referred to as 'final income'.

Examination skills

The skills most likely to be tested by examination questions on the distribution of income and wealth: poverty and inequality are as follows:

- Ability to distinguish between income and wealth and absolute and relative poverty.
- Interpreting data presented in the form of a Lorenz curve or a Gini coefficient.
- Knowledge of income and wealth inequalities and poverty in the UK and in developing economies.
- Distinguishing between equality and equity.
- Analysing how various government policies can affect poverty and the distribution of income and wealth.
- Evaluating the effectiveness of different policies aimed at reducing income and wealth inequalities and poverty.

Examination questions

Examination questions are likely to ask for description of inequalities in the distributions of income and/or wealth, explanation and analysis of the causes of identified inequalities, assessment of the implications of inequality for the UK economy, and/or evaluation of policies that governments use or might use to reduce inequality. MCQ 14 tests your understanding of the concept of relative poverty.

Common examination errors

Commonly made mistakes on income, wealth and poverty include:

- confusing income as a flow with wealth as a stock
- inability to explain and analyse inequalities and poverty in terms of market failure and government failure
- confusing equity with equality
- lack of understanding of how progressive taxes and transfers can, in principle, reduce inequality
- failing to apply supply and demand analysis and labour market theory to explain income inequality
- confusing absolute poverty and relative poverty.

Summary

- Income is an example of an economic flow whereas wealth is an example of an economic stock.
- In the UK, the distributions of income and wealth are both unequal, with the distribution of wealth being significantly more unequal.
- Different conditions in labour markets, differences between the unwaged and low-waged, and the nature of the welfare benefits system all provide explanations of income inequality.
- Horizontal equity involves treating people in the same circumstances equally, in contrast to vertical equity, which involves taking income from the rich on the grounds that they do not need it and redistributing this income to the poor on the grounds that they do need it.
- Absolute poverty and relative poverty are the two main poverty concepts.
- Progressive taxation and transfers are two government (fiscal) policies used to reduce both absolute and relative poverty.
- Low-waged workers may be caught in the poverty trap (or earnings trap), the immediate cause of which is the overlap between the income tax threshold and the means-tested welfare benefits ceiling.

The market mechanism, market failure and government intervention in markets

These notes, which relate to AQA specification section 4.1.8, prepare you to answer AQA examination questions on:

- how markets and prices allocate resources
- the meaning of market failure
- public goods, private goods and quasi-public goods
- positive and negative externalities in consumption and production
- merit and demerit goods
- market imperfections
- competition policy
- public ownership, privatisation, regulation and deregulation of markets
- government intervention in markets
- government failure.

Essential information

The advice offered in the following paragraphs builds on Topic 5 in Student Guide 1: *The operation of markets and market failure*. You should reread the relevant content of Student Guide 1 before proceeding with this topic in Student Guide 3.

How markets and prices allocate resources

Before reading any further, you should reread the section on page 35 of Student Guide 1 'How markets and prices allocate resources'. There we explained the signalling, incentive, rationing and allocative functions that prices perform in a market economy. You should also reread, starting on page 15 of Student Guide 1, Topic 3.1.2 on 'price determination in a competitive market'.

The meaning of market failure

Market failure occurs whenever the market mechanism or price mechanism performs unsatisfactorily, with the result that resource misallocation occurs.

There are two main ways in which markets fail. Markets can function inefficiently or they can function inequitably. It is also useful to distinguish between **complete market failure**, when the market simply does not exist, and **partial market failure**, when the market functions but produces the 'wrong' quantity of a good or service. In the former case, there is a **missing market**. In the latter case, the good or service may be provided too cheaply, in which case it is over-produced and over-consumed. Alternatively, as in monopoly, the good may be too expensive, in which case under-production and under-consumption result.

Public goods, private goods and quasi-public goods

Public goods divide into **pure public goods** and **quasi-public goods**. Pure public goods such as national defence exhibit the characteristics of **non-excludability** and **non-rivalry**, together with a third characteristic of **non-rejectability**.

Non-excludability means that it is impossible to provide a good to one person while preventing others from enjoying it. If the good is provided to one person, it is provided to all. National defence is an example.

Non-rivalry means that when a good is consumed by one person, it doesn't reduce the amount available for others. For example, when a person benefits from national defence, it does not prevent other people from experiencing similar benefits. By contrast, an item of food such as a strawberry is rival, because when one person eats the strawberry, nobody else can consume it.

With public goods, individuals face the temptation to consume or benefit without paying, or to free-ride. If enough people choose to free-ride, the incentive to provide the service through the market disappears – there is a missing market. Assuming that the majority of the country's inhabitants believe nuclear defence to be necessary (that is, a 'good' rather than a 'bad'), the market fails because it fails to provide a service for which there is a need. Public goods are thus associated with the **free-rider problem**. Free riding occurs when people decide to gain the benefits of a good or service while refusing to pay for it.

Many, perhaps most, public goods are quasi-public goods (or non-pure public goods) rather than pure public goods. This is often because various methods can be used to exclude free-riders. Non-pure public goods include roads, television and radio broadcasts, street lighting and lighthouses. In principle, roads can be converted into **private goods**, provided for profit through the market. This could be done by limiting points of access, by constructing toll gates or by introducing a scheme of electronic

Market failure When the price mechanism fails to allocate scarce resources in a productively efficient way and when the operation of market forces leads to an allocatively inefficient outcome and a net social welfare loss.

Complete market failure A market fails to function at all and a 'missing market' results.

Partial market failure A market functions, but it delivers the 'wrong' quantity of a good or service, which results in resource misallocation.

Missing market The absence of a market for a good or service, most commonly in the case of public goods and externalities.

Public good A good that exhibits the characteristics of non-excludability and non-rivalry.

Pure public good A good that is always non-excludable and non-rival.

Quasi-public good A good that has characteristics of both a public and a private good.

road pricing. However, the cost of making the good excludable may be very high, for example road pricing schemes on minor roads.

> **Private goods** Private goods possess the characteristics of excludability and rivalry.

Exam tip

Make sure you understand the difference between a public good and a quasi-public good and can give examples of both.

Public goods and allocative efficiency

The allocatively efficient or 'correct' quantity of any good produced and consumed is the quantity that people choose to consume when $P = MC$. However, in the case of a public good, assuming it is already being provided, the MC of providing the good to an extra consumer is zero. Allocative efficiency therefore occurs when $P = 0$ and the good is free for consumers. But private entrepreneurs willingly provide goods only if profit can be made, and for this to happen the price must be above zero ($P > 0$). In the case of a quasi-public good such as a road, this means that markets can provide a road only if the price of road use is set above the marginal cost of supply ($P > MC$). This reduces road use to below the allocatively efficient level. Hence, to achieve an allocatively efficient level of road use, motorists should not be charged for driving on the road, at least until the road becomes congested.

Positive and negative externalities in consumption and production

An **externality** is a special type of public good or public bad, which is dumped by those who produce it on **third parties** who receive or consume it, whether or not they choose to. Because externalities are generated and received outside the market, they provide examples of missing markets.

Externalities are classified in two main ways:

■ as negative externalities and positive externalities, also known as external costs and external benefits
■ as production externalities or as consumption externalities.

A **negative externality** is generated when an individual or firm making a decision to produce or consume a good or service does not have to pay the full cost of the decision. If the production of a good generates a negative externality, then the cost to society is greater than the cost incurred by the firm itself. Road congestion is a negative externality.

A **positive externality** is generated when an individual or firm making a decision does not receive the full benefit of the decision. The benefit to the individual or firm is less than the benefit to society. The pollination of fruit trees on neighbouring farms is a positive externality resulting from bee keeping.

Non-excludability A property of a public good which means that if it is provided for one person, it is provided for all.

Non-rivalry A property of a public good which means that when a good is consumed by one person, it does not reduce the amount available for others.

Non-rejectability A property of a public good which means that if the good is provided, it is impossible for a person to 'opt out' and not gain its benefits.

Free-rider problem Occurs when non-excludability leads to a situation in which not enough customers choose to pay for a good, preferring instead to free-ride.

Externality Occurs when production or consumption of goods or services imposes external costs or benefits on third parties outside of the market without these being reflected in market prices.

Third parties People affected by costs or benefits even though they do not choose to incur or receive the costs or benefits.

As is the case with public goods, the production and consumption of externalities leads to the free-rider problem. The provider of an external benefit such as a beautiful view cannot charge a market price to any willing free-riders who enjoy it. Conversely, the unwilling free-riders who receive or consume external costs such as pollution and noise cannot charge a price to the polluter for the bad that they reluctantly consume.

A **production externality** is generated, usually by firms, in the course of producing a good or service. By contrast, a **consumption externality** is generated by households and individuals in the course of consuming a good or service.

> **Production externality** When production of a good or a service imposes external costs or benefits on third parties outside of the market without these being reflected in market prices.

> **Consumption externality** When consumption of a good or a service imposes external costs or benefits on third parties outside of the market without these being reflected in market prices.

Merit goods and demerit goods

A **merit good**, such as education and health care, has two important characteristics: positive externalities in consumption and information problems which distort a consumer's choice on what is the privately optimal level of consumption.

When a person consumes a merit good such as health care, the resulting positive externalities benefit other people. An obvious example is that healthy people seldom spread diseases. The social benefit enjoyed by the wider community is greater than the private benefit enjoyed by the healthy person.

With regard to information problems, when deciding how much to consume, individuals take account of short-term costs and benefits, ignoring or undervaluing the long-term private costs and benefits. So whereas free-market provision leads to over-provision of a demerit good such as an alcoholic drink, it leads to under-provision of merit goods such as education and health care.

As is the case with a merit good, there are two main characteristics of a **demerit good** such as tobacco and alcoholic drinks. In the first place, when people consume demerit goods, they discharge negative externalities which are dumped on other people or third parties. The marginal social costs suffered by the wider community are greater than the marginal private costs incurred by a smoker or drinker. The second characteristic of a demerit good centres on the distinction between the short-term and the long-term private costs incurred by the person consuming the demerit good. For example, when teenagers first get the 'habit' of smoking, drinking or drug taking, may either ignore the long-term private costs they may suffer later in life, or downplay the significance of these costs. This behaviour illustrates an information problem.

These characteristics of demerit goods mean that free-market provision leads to market failure. Left to themselves, markets over-provide demerit goods.

> **Negative externality** A cost that is suffered by a third party as a result of production or consumption of a good or service.

> **Positive externality** A benefit that is enjoyed by a third party as a result of production or consumption of a good or service.

Exam tip

Make sure you can give examples of external costs and external benefits and are aware of the difference between production and consumption externalities.

> **Merit good** A good for which the social benefits of consumption exceed the social costs.

> **Demerit good** A good for which the social costs of consumption exceed the private costs.

Knowledge check 25

With examples, explain the difference between a public good and a merit good.

Market imperfections

Market failures are often the result of market imperfections, of course. In the case of merit goods and demerit goods we have just seen how imperfect and asymmetric information can lead to market failure. And as we shall explain shortly, the existence of monopoly and monopoly power can also lead to market failure. The immobility of factors of production such as capital and labour can also lead to regional inequalities, which are a form of market failure.

Many market imperfections and market failures can be analysed using the concepts of marginal private, external and social costs and benefits. Before we make use of these concepts, we shall first state a number of key definitions:

- Private benefit maximisation occurs when marginal private benefit (MPB) = marginal private cost (MPC).
- Social benefit maximisation, which maximises the public interest or the welfare of the whole community, occurs when marginal social benefit (MSB) = marginal social cost (MSC).
- Marginal social benefit (MSB) = marginal private benefit (MPB) + marginal external benefit (MEB).
- Marginal social cost (MSC) = marginal private cost (MPC) + marginal external cost (MEC).

Negative externalities and allocative inefficiency

Profit maximisation occurs in a perfect market at the price at which $P = MPC$. In the absence of externalities, this also means that the price equals the marginal social cost (MSC) of production: $P = MSC$. But when external costs are generated in the production of a good, $MSC > MPC$. So when $P = MPC$, $P < MSC$.

To achieve allocative efficiency, price must equal the *true* marginal cost of production: that is, the marginal social cost and not just the marginal private cost. But in a market situation, when externalities exist, the market mechanism fails to achieve an allocatively efficient outcome.

Using marginal analysis to show how negative production externalities cause market failure

Consider a fossil-fuel burning power station which, while producing electricity, discharges negative externalities but not positive externalities. In this situation, the marginal private benefit accruing to the power station from the production of electricity, and the marginal social benefit received by the whole community, are the same and shown by the downward-sloping curve in Figure 30. But, because pollution is discharged in the course of production, the marginal social cost of electricity production exceeds the marginal private cost incurred by the power station. In Figure 30, the MSC curve is positioned above the MPC curve. The vertical distance between two curves shows the marginal external cost (MEC) at each level of electricity production.

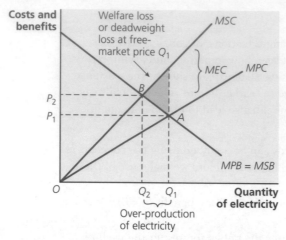

Figure 30 A coal-burning power station generating pollution (a negative production externality)

The power station maximises private benefit by producing output Q_1, where $MPC = MPB$. Q_1 is immediately below point A in Figure 30. However, the socially optimal level of output is Q_2, where $MSC = MSB$. Q_2 is immediately below point B. The shaded area illustrates the 'loss' of welfare or deadweight loss (DWL), which exists at the free-market output, Q_1 (where $MPC = MPB$), all the way back to the socially optimum output, Q_2.

Using marginal analysis to show how positive production externalities cause market failure

When positive production externalities are generated, the marginal social costs of production lie below the marginal private costs incurred by the producers of the good or service. This is illustrated in Figure 31, which shows the costs incurred when a commercial forestry company plants trees.

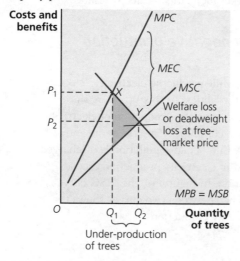

Figure 31 A commercial forestry company generating positive production externalities

Positive production externalities such as these mean that the *MSC* curve is positioned below the *MPC* curve. The vertical distance between the two curves shows a negative marginal external cost (*MEC*) at each level of tree planting. (A negative marginal external cost is exactly the same as a positive marginal external benefit enjoyed by society as a whole.)

Using marginal analysis to show how positive consumption externalities cause under-consumption of merit goods

Taking education as an example, when schooling is available only through the market, at prices unadjusted by subsidy, too little of the merit good ends up being consumed. In Figure 32, the privately optimal level of consumption is Q_1, determined at point A, where $MPC = MPB$. This is below the socially optimal level of consumption, Q_2.

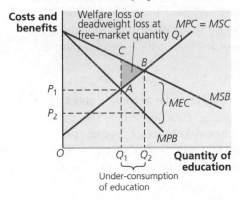

Figure 32 Under-consumption of a merit good in a free market

Using marginal analysis to show how negative consumption externalities cause over-consumption of demerit goods

Figure 33 shows that too much tobacco is being consumed when bought at market prices unadjusted by taxes or by a minimum price law. At least in the short term, the privately optimal level of consumption is Q_1, where $MPC = MPB$. This is greater than the socially optimal level of consumption, Q_2, located where $MSC = MSB$. Free-market provision of demerit goods therefore leads to over-consumption, and hence over-production.

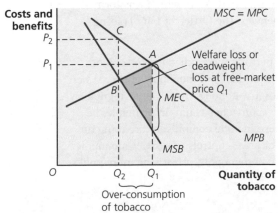

Figure 33 Over-consumption of a demerit good in a free market

> **Knowledge check 26**
>
> Distinguish between productive efficiency and allocative efficiency.

Why the absence of property rights leads to externalities in both production and consumption and hence market failure

Most goods in the economy are private goods for which the owners can exercise private property rights, which prevent other people from using the good or enjoying its benefits. By contrast, with pure public goods, the ownership of property rights cannot be exercised and this leads to their characteristic of non-excludability and the free-rider problem.

A well-functioning market economy requires the establishment and enforcement of well-defined property rights. Throughout history many people have lived close to rivers. On the one hand, rivers have provided vital drinking water, but on the other hand they provide a tempting way of disposing of waste. However, while being an important natural resource, for much of history rivers have been owned by nobody. As a result of the absence of property rights with regard to the ownership, for either consumption or disposal purposes, river water has tended to be polluted and overused.

Competition policy

As its name implies, **competition policy** is the part of government economic policy that tries to make the imperfectly competitive and monopolistic markets of the real world more competitive, and akin to the abstract model of perfect competition. The aims or objectives of competition policy include preventing the exploitation of monopoly power, efficiency, getting rid of excessive profit so that prices reflect costs of production, and the removal of entry and exit barriers that separate markets.

> **Competition policy**
> The part of the government's microeconomic policy and industrial policy that aims to make goods markets more competitive. It comprises policy regarding monopoly, mergers and restrictive trading practices.

However, competition policy does recognise that there are two main circumstances in which monopoly may be preferable to small firms producing in a competitive market. First, when the size of the market is limited but economies of scale are possible, monopolies can produce at a lower average cost than smaller, more competitive firms. Second, under certain circumstances, firms with monopoly power may be more innovative than firms that are not protected by entry barriers. When this is the case, monopoly may be more dynamically efficient than a more competitive market.

The Competition and Markets Authority

Since 2014, UK competition policy has been implemented on behalf of the government by the Competition and Markets Authority (CMA), which was formed through the merger of two older government agencies, the Office of Fair Trading (OFT) and the Competition Commission (CC).

The CMA uses market structure, conduct and performance indicators to scan or screen the UK economy on a systematic basis for evidence of monopoly abuse. When implementing competition policy, the CMA uses a 'watchdog investigatory/regulatory' approach. However, a number of other strategic approaches could, in principle, be used to deal with the problem of monopoly. These include compulsory breaking up of all monopolies ('monopoly busting'), the use of price controls to restrict monopoly abuse, rate of return regulation, state ownership of monopoly, privatising monopolies, and deregulation and the removal of barriers to entry.

Public ownership, privatisation, regulation and deregulation of markets

We have already mentioned these concepts in the context of possible ways to implement the government's competition policy. **Privatisation** involves the transfer of firms and businesses from **public ownership** or state ownership to the private sector.

Economic **regulation** involves the imposition of rules, controls and constraints, which restrict freedom of economic action in the market place. **Deregulation** is the opposite: the removal of previously imposed regulations. Governments use regulation to try to correct market failures and to achieve a socially optimal level of production and consumption. In the case of monopoly, regulation is used to limit and deter monopoly exploitation of consumers.

> **Exam tip**
>
> While there is a strong case for removing many regulations, for example those that unnecessarily raise costs of production and consumer prices, many regulations can be justified on the ground that they protect people from, for example, the abuse of monopoly power and harmful externalities.

Pro-free-market governments, including the current Conservative administration, generally prefer deregulation to ever more regulation. Deregulation is an important part of the Conservative government's policy of economic liberalisation.

Deregulation and the theory of contestable markets

Much of the justification for the policies of deregulation and economic liberalisation that have been pursued in recent years has been provided by the theory of contestable markets. Contestable market theory argues that the most effective way to promote competitive behaviour within markets is not to impose ever more regulation upon firms and industries, but to carry out the opposite process of deregulation. According to this view, the main function of deregulation is to remove barriers to entry, thereby creating incentives both for new firms to enter and contest the market and for established firms to behave in a more competitive way.

Regulatory capture

Another theory that has had some influence upon the trend towards deregulation is the theory of **regulatory capture**. This theory argues that regulatory agencies created by government can be 'captured' by the industries or firms they are intended to oversee and regulate. Following capture, the regulatory agencies begin to operate in the industry's interest rather than on behalf of the consumers they are supposed to protect.

Even if regulatory capture does not take place, the supporters of deregulation argue that much regulatory activity is unnecessary and ultimately burdensome upon industry and consumers. Once established, the regulators have an incentive to extend their role by introducing ever more rules and regulations, since it is in this way that they justify their pay and their jobs. Regulation acts both as an informal 'tax' upon the regulated, raising production costs and consumer prices, and as an extra barrier to market entry, restricting competition.

Privatisation The transfer of assets from public ownership to private ownership.

Public ownership Firms and industries owned by government.

Regulation Imposing, often by law, rules that limit people's freedom of action.

Deregulation The removal of previously imposed regulations.

Knowledge check 28

Distinguish between privatisation and deregulation.

Regulatory capture Occurs when regulatory agencies act in the interest of regulated firms rather than on behalf of the consumers they are supposed to protect.

Government intervention in markets

Governments can intervene in markets in two main ways: through regulation and through imposing taxes, for example to discourage consumption of a demerit good or encourage consumption of a merit good. Other forms of intervention include maximum and minimum price laws (price ceilings and price floors) and the creation of markets in permits to pollute.

In a permits to pollute scheme, maximum limits are imposed on the amount of pollution that industries are allowed to emit, followed by a steady reduction in each subsequent year (say, by 5%) of the maximum amount. Once this regulatory framework has been established, a market in traded pollution permits takes over, creating market-orientated incentives for firms to reduce pollution because they can make money out of it.

The government can also enforce legal entitlement to private property rights. If the law provides people with the property right to breathe unpolluted air, breach of this right enables victims to sue polluting companies for financial compensation. To avoid having to pay financial compensation, polluters would have to take action to eliminate the discharge of negative externalities. Alternatively, if it is impossible to eliminate a negative externality without simultaneously eliminating production of the good that produces the externality, polluters could offer people money to sign away the right to breathe unpolluted air. Either way, if the externality persists, the people who suffer pollution receive financial compensation.

Government failure

Whereas market failure occurs when markets function inefficiently or inequitably, **government failure** can occur when government intervention to try to reduce or eliminate a market failure has the unintended consequence of creating a new problem or problems. If the government failure is greater than the market failure that the government intervention was intended to correct, it is better to leave the market failure uncorrected and to live with it.

Examination skills

The skills most likely to be tested by objective-test and data-response questions on the market mechanism, market failure and government intervention in markets are as follows:
- Explaining the meaning of market failure and government failure.
- Distinguishing between private goods, public goods and quasi-public goods.
- Explaining market failure in the contexts of externalities and demerit and merit goods with the application of marginal analysis.
- Analysing market failures using the concept of allocative efficiency
- Explaining how a monopoly may adversely affect resource allocation.
- Identifying the different ways in which governments can intervene in markets to correct market failures.
- Using the concept of property rights to distinguish between public and private ownership.
- Distinguishing between regulation and deregulation.
- Appreciating that government intervention may not be successful and that problems of government failure may result.

Government failure
When government intervention in the economy makes the allocation of resources worse. The intervention may be ineffective, or wasteful and/or damaging.

Exam tip
Government failure often results from the unintended consequences of interventionist policies that were introduced in an attempt to correct market failure.

Examination questions

Examination questions are likely to be set on all three components of this topic. MCQs 11 and 12 respectively test your understanding of environmental market failures and government intervention in markets. DRQ 1 on competition and monopoly in the EU domestic airline industry touches indirectly on competition policy. The investigation question at the end of the Student Guide encompasses market failure, government failure and methods of government intervention that could reduce the problem of freshwater flooding in the UK.

Common examination errors

Commonly made mistakes on the market mechanism, market failure and government intervention in markets are:

- failure to explain how and why the market fails in the case of public goods and externalities
- naively assuming that government intervention always succeeds in correcting market failure
- failure to understand that markets can produce merit and demerit goods, but they produce the 'wrong' quantity
- describing methods of government intervention when a question asks for evaluation of methods
- inability to apply marginal analysis and to draw correctly diagrams illustrating marginal social, external and private costs and benefits
- failure to appreciate the many different ways in which governments can intervene, including state ownership and direct provision of goods and services.

Summary

- Market failure occurs whenever the market mechanism or price mechanism performs unsatisfactorily, either inequitably or inefficiently.
- You should refer back to Student Guide 1 to remind yourself of some of the principal market failures: public goods, externalities, and merit and demerit goods.
- Public goods divide into pure and quasi-public goods.
- The main 'add-on' topics for understanding market failure in Student Guide 3 are the application of marginal analysis and the concept of allocative efficiency to market failure, and the case for extending private property rights.

- Government failure occurs when government intervention in markets to try to correct market failure is ineffective or damaging.
- Competition policy, public ownership and regulation are three examples of government intervention in markets.
- The regulation of market activity can lead to the problem of regulatory capture.
- Deregulation reflects the impact of the theory of contestable markets.
- You must avoid confusing government failure with market failure.

Questions & Answers

A-level Paper 1

At A-level, the 'Markets and market failure' Paper 1 is 2 hours long and has a maximum mark of 80. The exam paper contains two sections, A and B, both of which must be answered. Section A, which accounts for 40 marks (50% of the total), comprises two data-response questions (DRQs), labelled Context 1 and Context 2, of which you should answer one. Section B, which also accounts for 40 marks (50% of the total), contains three essay questions (EQs), of which you should answer one. Essays account for 50% of total assessment in the A-level Paper 1 and Paper 2 exams.

A-level Paper 3

Besides including a case study investigation, the A-level Paper 3 exam has 30 MCQs, of which roughly half are on microeconomics, with the others being on macroeconomics. The MCQs that follow in this guide, which are all on microeconomics, are similar to those in the A-level Paper 3 exam. The MCQs in Section A of Paper 3 are followed in Section B of Paper 3 by extended-response questions based on a case study, which require a student to draw together different areas of the specification. An 'extended response' is evidence generated by a student which is of sufficient length to allow that student to demonstrate the ability to construct and develop a sustained line of reasoning that is coherent, relevant, substantiated and logically structured. The case study in Part B is not pre-released.

The assessment objectives

Assessment objectives (AOs) are set by a government agency, Ofqual, and are the same across the AS and A-level economics specifications. The exams measure how students have achieved the following assessment objectives:

- AO1: Demonstrate knowledge of terms/concepts and theories/models to show an understanding of the behaviour of economic agents (consumers, workers and firms) and how they are affected by and respond to economic issues. Weighting: at A-level 20–23%.

- AO2: Apply knowledge and understanding to various economic contexts to show how economic agents are affected by and respond to economic issues. Weighting: at A-level 26–29%.

- AO3: Analyse issues within economics, showing an understanding of their impact on economic agents. Weighting: at A-level 26–29%.

- AO4: Evaluate economic arguments and use qualitative and quantitative evidence to support informed judgements relating to economic issues. Weighting: at A-level 22–25%.

- AO1 and AO2 are testing 'lower-order' skills, whereas AO3 and AO4 test 'higher-order' skills.

The exam questions in this guide

This guide includes 21 examination-style questions designed to be a key learning, revision and exam preparation resource. We start off with 15 multiple-choice questions (MCQs), which reflects the fact that approximately half of the MCQs in Part A of Paper 3 at A-level are set on microeconomic topics, with the remaining 15 being set on macroeconomic topics, which are covered in Student Guide 4.

The MCQs are followed by two data-response questions (DRQs) and three essay questions (EQs). Each of these questions is similar to those set in A-level Paper 1. The first DRQ or Context question is followed by four sub-parts to the question: 01, 02, 03 and 04, with the maximum marks for each sub-part being 01: 2 marks, 02: 4 marks, 03: 9 marks and 04: 25 marks. The second DRQ or Context question is followed by four sub-parts, numbered 05, 06, 07 and 08.

The two parts of the first essay question are numbered 09 and 10. The two parts of the second essay question are numbered 11 and 12, and the two parts of the third essay question are numbered 13 and 14.

Part B of Paper 3 contains a single case study or investigation question. The question starts off with a scenario, which 'sets the scene' for the question. Students will be asked to use selected information in the three or so extracts in the question, and also their general knowledge, to write answers written in the style of an economist providing advice to a client. The client could be, among others, a government department, a local authority, a regulatory body, a trade body or a trade union. Because the investigation in Part B of Paper 3 follows the 30 MCQs in Part A, the three sub-parts of the question are numbered 31, 32 and 33. The maximum marks for the three sub-parts to the question will be: 31: 10 marks, 32: 15 marks and 33: 25 marks.

Students reading this guide could use the questions for revision purposes. All the questions can be used 'en bloc' as part of a short trial or mock exam near the end of your course. Alternatively, as you study a topic in the Content Guidance section of this guide, you could refer selectively to particular questions in this section that assess aspects of the topic.

This section of the Student Guide also contains:
■ correct answers for the MCQs
■ comments on the MCQs, explaining particular features of each question
■ a student answer to each of the DRQs and to the investigation question
■ comments on each student's answer explaining, where relevant, how the answer could be improved, even though, as it stands, it is already a grade A* (or A) or C standard answer. These comments are denoted by the icon **ⓔ** .

■ Multiple-choice questions

Note: the 15 multiple-choice questions that follow provide examples of questions typical of those set in Part A of Paper 3 in the A-level examination. Each MCQ is followed by a short guidance note. The correct answers, along with brief explanatory notes, follow on from the questions.

Question 1 Economic methodology

Hypothesis testing is used by economists:

A To test natural laws.

B In the development of economic theories.

C As a part of inductive reasoning.

D To prove that economic theories are true.

ⓔ This is typical of questions you should expect on economic methodology.

Question 2 Utility

Utility is:

A A measure of the economic welfare enjoyed in consumption by households.

B Enjoyed solely from the consumption of inferior goods.

C Always positive.

D The same as normal profit.

ⓔ A question that tests understanding of the meaning of a key concept in demand theory.

Question 3 Behavioural economics

Behavioural economists generally assume that:

A Firms always aim to maximise profit.

B Governments can successfully influence people to change their behaviour.

C Members of households are never influenced by altruism.

D Consumers always act to maximise utility.

ⓔ When answering a question such as this, look out for deterministic words such as 'always' and 'never'.

Question 4 Production theory

Which of the following is a true statement relating to production theory?

A Short-run production theory is the same as short-run cost theory.

B Only long-run production theory can be used to explain revenue curves.

C Short-run and long-run production theories respectively help to explain short-run and long-run cost curves.

D Decreasing returns to scale are a feature of short-run production theory.

ⓔ This question is inviting you to confuse short-run and long-run production theory.

Question 5 Cost curves

A mobile phone company finds that its total costs are best illustrated by the following curve.

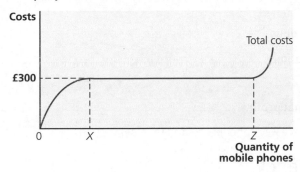

What can be deduced about costs over the range of output from *X* to *Z*?

A Average costs are rising.

B Marginal costs are £300 and constant.

C Total costs are rising.

D Marginal costs are zero.

ⓔ This question is testing your understanding of the link between marginal and total costs.

Question 6 Revenue and profit

Having changed from a policy of profit maximisation to one of revenue maximisation, a monopoly is now likely be operating at a:

A Higher level of output and higher marginal revenue.

B Lower level of output but with marginal revenue equal to marginal cost.

C Higher level of output and lower marginal costs.

D Higher level of output and lower marginal revenue.

ⓔ This question is testing your knowledge and understanding of marginal concepts.

Question 7 Competitive markets

In a perfectly competitive industry, there are:

A Many buyers and many sellers.

B Many sellers, but there might be only one or two buyers.

C Many buyers, but there might be only one or two sellers.

D Many sellers, but one firm that sets the price for the others to follow.

(e) This question is testing your knowledge and understanding of the six conditions of perfect competition.

Question 8 Contestable markets

To minimise the chance of entry by new competitors in a highly contestable market, incumbent firms should:

A Set their prices to make normal profit only.

B Abandon any forms of price discrimination.

C Agree to cooperate with each other.

D Raise their prices to maximise abnormal profit.

(e) Normal profit and price discrimination are key concepts tested in this question.

Question 9 Economic efficiency

Assuming there are no externalities and no economies or diseconomies of scale, which of the following would always be true for a profit-maximising firm operating in a perfectly competitive market?

A The firm is productively efficient in the short run but not the long run.

B The firm is productively efficient in both the short run and the long run.

C The firm is allocatively efficient in the long run but not necessarily productively efficient in the short run.

D The firm is allocatively efficient in the short run but not the long run.

(e) Efficiency criteria and welfare criteria provide the two main ways in which the 'good' and 'bad' features of different market structures are evaluated. This question is about efficiency criteria.

Question 10 Consumer surplus

Which of the following statements about consumer surplus is correct?

A Only wealthy consumers can enjoy consumer surplus.

B Consumer surplus is the same as entrepreneurial profit.

C Consumer surplus is gained when households pay a price for a good that is less than the highest price that they would be willing to pay.

D Consumer surplus is gained when firms charge a price that is higher than the lowest price that they would be willing to accept.

(e) This question is about welfare criteria.

Question 11 Environmental market failure

The following graph shows the possible distances driven by a firm's delivery lorry on a particular day.

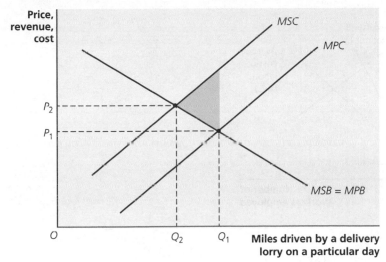

With reference to the graph, which of the following statements is correct?

A The shaded area shows the general public's welfare gain when the lorry's journey length is Q_1.

B A price of P_2 charged for delivery may lead to a socially optimal outcome.

C Negative consumption externalities are being generated.

D The delivery company should charge customers a price of P_1 to correct any possible environmental market failure.

e This question is testing your understanding of a range of concepts related to market failure.

Question 12 Government intervention in markets

All the following statements about government intervention in markets are correct except one. Which statement is incorrect?

A Governments never intervene in markets in mixed economies.

B Government intervention often aims to correct market failures.

C Government intervention is not necessarily successful.

D Government intervention sometimes leads to government failure.

e Students often confuse government failure with market failure.

Question 13 Labour markets

The following figure shows a labour market in equilibrium with a wage rate of W_1 and a level of employment of L_1.

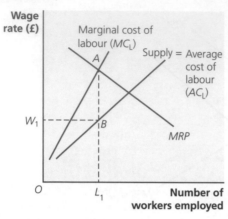

It can be inferred from the figure that:

A   This is a perfectly competitive labour market.

B   Point A determines the level of employment but not the wage rate.

C   Labour market equilibrium occurs when the marginal revenue product of labour equals the wage rate.

D   There is no evidence of the exercise of market power in the labour market.

ⓔ Although the word is not mentioned in the question, this is a question about monopsony.

Question 14 Poverty

Relative poverty is usually defined as:

A   A condition characterised by severe deprivation of basic human needs.

B   Occurring at all hourly wage rates below the national living wage.

C   Occurring when income is below a specified proportion of average income.

D   The state of being extremely poor.

ⓔ This question is inviting you to confuse relative poverty with absolute poverty.

Question 15 Competition policy

All the following statements about current competition policy in the UK are correct except one. Which statement is incorrect?

A   The Competition and Markets Authority implements current UK competition policy.

B   Competition policy deals with monopolies, mergers and trading restrictive practices.

C   Competition policy tries to ensure that dominant firms act in the public interest.

D   Competition policy deals with labour restrictive practices.

ⓔ MCQs require you to select a correct answer and to separate it from three incorrect statements, which are known as distractors. However, some questions like this one ask you to choose an incorrect statement, given that the other three statements are correct.

Answers to multiple-choice questions

Question 1

Statement **B** is the correct answer because hypotheses are tested in the development of economic theories. Statement **A** is wrong because physical science and not economic science is used to test natural laws. Statement **C** is wrong because deductive rather than inductive reasoning is used to test hypotheses. Finally, Statement **D** is wrong because testing seeks to falsify or refute a hypothesis rather than to prove its truth.

Question 2

Statement **A** is the correct answer. Utility shows the satisfaction, pleasure or fulfilment of need, all of which relate to economic welfare, enjoyed in consumption. The 'weasel word' *solely* makes Statement **B** incorrect. Utility can be negative (disutility), so Statement **C** is wrong, and Statement **D** is wrong because utility has nothing to do with normal profit.

Question 3

Statement **B** is the correct answer – behavioural economists do indeed assume that governments can successfully influence people to change their behaviour. Statement **A**, which could be true for many, though not all, traditional economists, is incorrect in this context. Finally, the 'weasel words' *never* and *always* render Statements **C** and **D** incorrect.

Question 4

Statement **C** is the correct answer. Statement **B** invites you to confuse production theory and cost theory, while Statement **A** involves similar confusion of returns and revenue. Finally, Statement **D** is wrong because returns to scale are a feature of long-run rather than short-run production theory.

Question 5

Between points X and Z, total costs are unchanged, so the marginal cost of producing an extra unit of output must be zero. This means that Statement **D** is correct. Since at zero, with $MC < AC$, average costs must be falling, Statement **A** is wrong. While marginal costs are constant, they are constant at zero rather than at £300; Statement **B** is therefore wrong. Finally, the graph shows that total costs are constant, so they can't be rising. This means that Statement **C** is wrong.

Question 6

Statement **D** is the correct answer. At the profit-maximising level of output, $MR = MC$. Since MC is positive, MR is also positive. However, at the revenue-maximising level of output, $MR = 0$. This means that with a falling MR curve, output increases but MR falls compared with the profit-maximising level of output. None of the other statements (**A**, **B** or **C**) captures this.

Question 7

Many buyers and sellers is one of the conditions of perfect competition, so Statement **A** is correct. None of the other statements (**B**, **C** or **D**) is true for perfect competition.

Question 8

In a highly contestable market, new firms can easily enter the market. However, if incumbent firms are making only normal profit, the incentive to enter the market disappears. This means that Statement **A** is the correct answer. Statement **D** is stating the opposite to Statement A and is therefore wrong. Statements **B** and **C** are irrelevant to the question.

Question 9

Statement **C** is the correct answer. Allocative efficiency requires that $P = MC$ and this is true in perfect competition in both the short run and the long run. But while the firm will be minimising average costs and thus will be productively efficient in the long run, this is unlikely to be the case in the short run. None of the other statements (**A**, **B** or **D**) is correct.

Question 10

Statement **C** is correct, setting out what happens when consumers enjoy consumer surplus. Statement **D** invites you to confuse consumer and producer surplus, while Statements **A** and **B** are simply muddled.

Question 11

Statement **B** is correct, since the socially optimal outcome occurs when $MSB = MSC$. Statement **A** is wrong because the shaded area shows a welfare loss when the lorry's journey length is Q_1. Statement **C** is wrong because production rather than consumption externalities are being generated. Statement **D** is wrong because price P_2 rather than P_1 should be charged.

Question 12

All the statements are true except Statement **A**, which is thus the correct answer. 'Never' is the give-away word in Statement A – governments often intervene in mixed economies.

Question 13

Statement **B** is the correct answer. The level of employment is determined at point A where $MRP = MC_L$, but the wage rate is determined at point B, where $W = AC_L$. Statement **C** is wrong because it confuses these two equations. The upward-sloping MC_L and AC_L curves tell us that this is a monopsony labour market, so Statement **A** is wrong. In monopsony, there is evidence of market power, so Statement **D** is wrong.

Question 14

Statement **C** provides a correct definition of relative policy and thus is the answer. Statement **A** is a definition of absolute poverty and not relative poverty, so is therefore wrong. Statement **B** might lead to relative poverty, but it is not a definition of the concept. Finally, Statement **D** gives a definition of poverty but not of relative poverty.

Question 15

Statements **A**, **B** and **C** are all correct. Statement **D**, which invites you to confuse trading restrictive practices with labour restrictive practices, is the only incorrect statement. This means that Statement D is the answer to this question.

■Data-response questions

Note: the two data-response questions that follow provide examples of questions typical of those set in Part A of Paper 1 in the A-level examination. Each part of the questions is followed by a short guidance note. A student answer, along with examiner comments, follows on from the questions.

Context 1
Competition and monopoly in the EU airline industry

Total for this context: 40 marks

Study Extracts A, B and C, then answer the questions that follow.

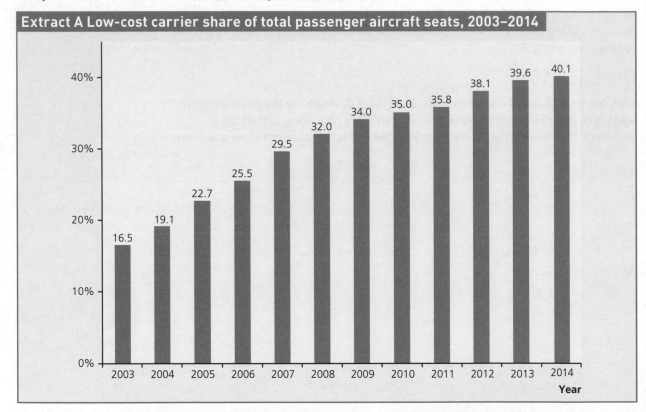

Extract A Low-cost carrier share of total passenger aircraft seats, 2003–2014

Year	Value
2003	16.5
2004	19.1
2005	22.7
2006	25.5
2007	29.5
2008	32.0
2009	34.0
2010	35.0
2011	35.8
2012	38.1
2013	39.6
2014	40.1

Extract B Air France and British Airways and competition in their domestic markets

At present, the most dominant airline in a domestic market in the European Union is Air France, which has 80% of seat capacity in the domestic market in France. (A country's domestic market is restricted to flights to and from airports within the country, 5 but does not include flights to and from other EU countries.) Air France is eight times bigger than its nearest rival, the low-cost carrier (LCC) easyJet, in the French domestic air market.

Market dominance gives Air France considerable 10 monopoly power in the market for domestic flights. However, Air France claims that its 'dominance' is not as great as it seems because it faces competition, not from rival airlines but from France's TGV high-speed rail network. Because 15 of this, the airline argues, travellers have ample choice and are not exploited by abuse of Air France's monopoly power.

Unlike Air France, which has determinedly hung on to its dominant position in the French market, British Airways ranks only third in the UK domestic market, well behind low-cost carriers Flybe and easyJet. Some economists believe that the main reason for the difference between Air France's dominant position in the domestic French market and BA's minority position in the UK market lies in the fact that Britain conforms to the spirit of the Single European Market (SEM) while France does not. The SEM is meant to allow completely free competition in all industries and markets and in all 28 member states. Clearly, such competition does not exist and countries such as the UK that allow firms from other EU countries to compete freely in their domestic markets are the ones that suffer.

Source: News reports, 2013

Extract C EU airlines fined over cartel

The European Commission initially fined 11 airlines almost €800 million for fixing the price of air cargo between 1999 and 2006. The EU Competition Commissioner said that the 'deplorable' cartel 'would have continued, harming both companies and consumers', had the EU not intervened. British Airways was fined €104 million, Air France–KLM €340 million and Cargolux Airlines €79.9 million.

The EU said that the airlines 'coordinated their action on surcharges for fuel and contacted each other so as to ensure that worldwide air freight carriers imposed a flat rate surcharge per kilogram for all shipments'.

'With today's decision the Commission is sending a clear message that it will not tolerate cartel behaviour,' the Commissioner said. The German carrier Lufthansa escaped a fine because it alerted the regulatory authorities to the cartel.

However, in 2015, following an appeal by the 11 airlines involved in the case, the General Court of the European Union said there were 'internal inconsistencies' in the European Commission's 2010 decision to fine airlines. The airlines thus eventually escaped punishment.

Source: News reports, 2010–2015

[01] Using the data in Extract A, calculate the median market share of low-cost carrier passenger aircraft seats in Europe over the years between 2002 and 2014. [2 marks]

e Make sure you don't confuse two measures of an average: the mean and the median.

[02] Explain whether the data in Extract A suggest that the market power of large airlines increased in Europe over the data period. [4 marks]

e This question contains the words 'market power'. Is this the same as the terms 'market dominance' and 'monopoly power' mentioned in the part [03] question?

[03] Extract B lines 10–11 state 'Market dominance gives Air France considerable monopoly power in the market for domestic flights.'

With the help of a diagram, analyse how Air France might use its monopoly power in the market for domestic flights in France to exploit airline passengers. [9 marks]

e Be careful of the word 'exploit'. Explain in your answer what you think the word might mean.

[04] 'Decisions by firms to cooperate with each other are always against the public interest.'

Evaluate this statement and assess the view that cartels, such as the airline cartel mentioned in Extract C, should be investigated and policed solely by national competition authorities such as the UK Competition and Markets Authority, and not by the European Union competition authorities.

[25 marks]

@ There are two parts to this question, but both are testing the skill of evaluation. The first part of your answer must consider the meaning of 'the public interest'. Your answer to the second part should be improved if you understand the meaning of the word 'subsidiarity'. This involves the delegation of cartel policy as much as possible to national governments.

Student answer

[01] There are 12 values in Extract A from which the median value is calculated. This means that with an even number of values, the middle two must be selected and then averaged. The middle two values are 32% and 34%, for which the average is 33%. The median market share of low-cost carrier passenger aircraft seats between 2002 and 2014 was thus 33%.

@ **2/2 marks awarded.** A correct and fully explained calculation, which earns both marks. Even though in this case the explanation is not needed, it could still pick up a mark if there was a slip in the calculation.

[02] The data in Extract A suggest that the European airline market has become more competitive in recent years as low-cost airlines have taken a greater share of passenger seats from the traditional airline carriers. In 2003, the low-cost airlines accounted for only 16.5% of the total passenger seats, but in every year shown the low-cost airlines increased their share of the market. By the end of the period their share of seats had increased by 40.1%. This means that the low-cost airlines have taken a significant number of passengers from the traditional airlines in the 11-year period.

@ **3/4 marks awarded.** The answer shows a good understanding of the issue posed by the question but loses a mark for making a slight slip when stating the market share of the small airlines had increased by 40.1% rather than to 40.1%. Also, the answer does not state explicitly that the market power of large airlines has not increased, stating instead that the European airline market has become more competitive in recent years. It amounts to the same thing, but it is better to use the wording in the question.

[03] The European Commission defines a monopoly as any situation when a firm controls 25% or more of the market share in a given market. Air France has a dominant position in the domestic flights market in France because it has '80% of seat capacity', according to Extract B. Hence Air France can be described as having been able to behave like a monopoly because of the lack of competition in the market.

The effect of market dominance is illustrated in the figure below, which is a standard monopoly profit diagram.

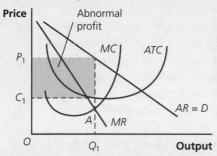

Air France will be able to exercise monopoly power and set a high price, shown on the diagram at P_1. A monopoly will choose to set the price at this point because it is where the revenue received from the sale of the last seat is equal to the cost of providing the seat, enabling Air France to maximise profit. Due to the existence of barriers to entry, competition will find it difficult to enter the market. Hence, customers have to either pay the high price set by the airline or go without the service. The monopoly will make abnormal profits selling at P_1 because it will cost only C_1 to provide the flights. This price and level of output are inefficient and do not maximise social welfare, but passengers have to pay the high price even if they feel exploited by Air France.

@ **8/9 marks awarded.** The answer starts with a slight error: the 25% market share definition of monopoly has been one used by the UK competition authorities but not by the European Commission. The European Commission defines monopoly in a rather vague manner in terms of dominant firms behaving in an anti-competitive way. However, under the principle of subsidiarity, the EU delegates much of competition policy, including the local definition of monopoly, to national authorities such as the Competition and Markets Authority. However, apart from this error, which is not important, we have judged this answer to reach the mid-point in Level 3 (7–9 marks). Level 3 is the highest level in the mark scheme for the third part of a data-response question.

[04] The fundamental purpose of an economic system is to efficiently allocate resources in a manner that maximises human welfare. Government officials can, therefore, be acting in the public interest if they are seeking to ensure that markets are working more efficiently and improving the living standards of citizens. The nature and objectives of competition policy raise extremely important issues at both the British and European level. At present the British government and the European Commission can investigate and fine firms that are deemed to be acting in an anti-competitive manner but at the same time allow firms to cooperate and enjoy monopoly power in industries such as pharmaceuticals. Economic theory offers justifications for these contradictory policy decisions, but they can also appear to be based on normative assumptions.

Traditional economic theory teaches that markets normally work best when competition is fierce. The model of perfect competition provides an abstract theory that allows economists to imagine how markets would behave if competition could truly thrive. It shows that waste and inefficiency are eliminated in the long run because competition will drive prices down and force businesses to offer consumers the best product at the lowest price. Hence, economists should object to any decision by firms to cooperate when making output decisions and setting prices. In markets where significant economies of scale exist, such as the airline industry, competition should still be encouraged. Large oligopolies such as Air France and BA should compete to offer passengers the best flights at the lowest price. Collusion and cartel price fixing should be punished with significant fines like the ones reported in Extract C and imposed by the European Commission.

In this situation price-fixing cooperation between large firms is not in the public interest because the motivation driving the firms' behaviour is profit maximisation. The high prices will not have any long-term benefits for consumers or society, they will only enable the airlines to enjoy excessive profits at the expense of passengers. High prices are inefficient because not enough of society's resources are allocated to the production of the good and human living standards are not maximised.

If firms engage in anti-competitive behaviour in the UK, it is appropriate for the British competition authorities to investigate and sanction businesses that break British laws. It does not make sense for the European Commission to intervene in matters that only relate to the British economy. In the case of international airlines, it makes sense, however, for the European Commission to investigate and fine firms that collude across the legal jurisdictions of national governments but inside the European Single Market. The UK is a member of the EU and the SEM. The European Commission is better placed than the UK competition authorities to deal with oligopolies that operate across national boundaries because it can investigate firms' behaviour in different countries. As can be seen in Extract C, cartels in the airline industry can include companies such as British Airways, Air France–KLM, Cargolux and Lufthansa. When collusion is organised by multinational corporations across Europe, then the European competition authorities are better placed to deal with oligopolies than national governments.

However, the practice of cooperation between firms is not always against the public interest. Oligopolistic pharmaceutical firms have been allowed to cooperate in the past so that they share research and development costs in order to create new drugs and treatments for disease. Governments then allow these firms to enjoy patent protection and establish monopoly power, enabling them to enjoy abnormal profits for up to 20 years. Although consumers may endure high prices, they significantly benefit from the creation of ground-breaking medical advancements. In this situation the benefits of cooperation and high prices outweigh the costs because both individuals and society have access to new products that would not have otherwise been developed. Hence cooperation can foster innovation and increase human welfare.

My conclusion is that, ultimately, competition authorities need to make decisions that are in the public interest and operate in the legal jurisdiction that is most appropriate to the situation. Competitive oligopoly is the most desirable situation in most markets. Hence, governments should prohibit cooperation among firms and punish offending firms with hefty fines. However, if cooperation is necessary to foster the environment for innovations that bring significant advancements, then competition policy should allow firms to work together and if successful, enjoy monopoly profits.

@ **23/25 marks awarded.** This is an excellent, if rather discursive, answer which reaches the mid-point of the highest Level 5 (21–25) in the mark scheme for the final part of a data-response question testing the skills of developed analysis and evaluation. The answer displays sound, focused analysis and well-supported evaluation that is well organised, showing sound knowledge and understanding of economic terminology, concepts and principles, with few, if any, errors. It includes well-focused analysis with clear, logical chains of reasoning and also supported evaluation throughout the response and in the conclusion.

@ **Total score: 36/40 = Grade A***

Context 2

EU labour migration and the UK

Total for this context: 40 marks

Study Extracts D, E and F, and then answer all parts of the questions that follow.

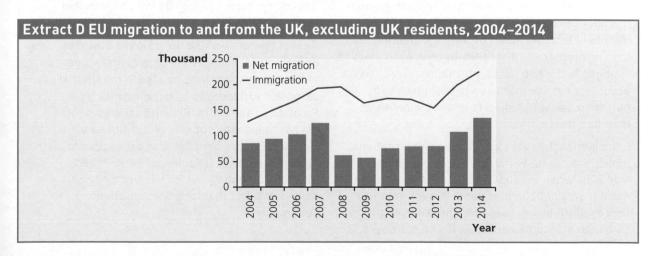

Extract D EU migration to and from the UK, excluding UK residents, 2004–2014

Extract E Is net migration from Poland into Britain coming to an end?

Back at the beginning of 2007, Kris Ploski employed 50 Polish builders working in his construction firm. By the end of 2007, that had suddenly changed. 'It hit me hard,' said Ploski. 'Nearly 30% of my team didn't come back after Christmas.' From agriculture to construction you will find a similar story. [5]

So why were Poles forsaking high wages, guaranteed employment and bad weather for a less certain future back home? One expert says the decision is mostly down to simple economics [10] and how this affects those Polish migrants (most of them) who send a proportion of their earnings home. Official statistics showed that a combination of recession and a plummeting pound – which [15] reduced the value of remittances home – led to a record emigration from the UK of Poles and other workers from the new EU member states in central Europe.

At the time, a spokesman for the Institute for Public Policy Research had asked: 'What [20] will happen to the UK economy if these large numbers of Poles stop coming?' In sectors such as farming and food processing, he warned, there are serious questions about how they will [25] remain sustainable if the labour supply dries up. The farm sector would be in dire straits without the immigrants willing to do the hard graft on the land. But in agriculture, the typical worker's overtime pay fell sharply at the time [30] that migrants began to work on farms. In hotels and restaurants, basic pay fell, too. One local man coming out of the dole office said: 'I'd prefer to sign on than do the jobs that migrant workers do.' [35]

Is a Polish exodus good news for British workers? Some business leaders believe the Poles have allowed us to paper over fundamental problems within our economy. The chief executive of the British Chambers of [40] Commerce said: 'There is an attitude and work ethic problem in certain parts of the UK, where people do not see the need or have the desire to work.'

Source: adapted from news sources

Extract F The effects of European Union enlargement

Enlargement of the European Union has created a much larger internal market, which has led to both trade creation and trade diversion. Trade creation increases the total volume of international trade because the growth of internal free trade among [5] members exceeds any loss of trade with non-members brought about by tariffs protecting the trading bloc. Trade diversion, by contrast, refers to changes in the pattern of international trade which occur when trade that used to take place with [10] non-member states diverts into trade between member states.

Enlargement has also increased the international mobility of labour within the European Union. After May 2004 when Poland joined the European Union, [15] more than 600,000 Poles came to work in the UK. Scores of UK businesses then thrived from the £4 billion of income earned by Polish plumbers, builders, bar staff, waiters, nannies and other migrant workers. In response, some of the [20] biggest names in British business began to 'go Polish'. For example, the supermarket group J Sainsbury started selling 32 Polish foods and since 2009 this number has grown substantially.

'At last they are waking up,' said the business [25] development manager of Polish Express, one of the eight newspapers printed in the UK that came into existence to target migrants from Poland. 'To start with, British businesses just did not realise the opportunities.' But now [30] Barclays Bank is bending over backwards to attract customers from the growing Polish migrant community, which has become just as important as that for any other ethnic community. [35]

However, migration from countries such as Poland imposes costs upon the UK economy, which may have to be paid for through higher tax rates. A small number of schools saw a significant increase in admissions. Some local authorities reported problems of overcrowding in private housing. There have been cost pressures on English language training.

So what impact has the Polish consumer had on British businesses? 'It was basically like 45 adding the consumer demand of Liverpool to the economy in just two years,' said the chief 40 executive of the Centre for Economics and Business Research, a think tank.

Source: adapted from news sources

[05] Using Extract D, calculate to two decimal places the percentage change in immigration into the UK over the period shown. [2 marks]

ⓔ The danger when answering this question is confusing changes in immigration with changes in net migration: that is, immigration minus emigration.

[06] Explain why the net migration figures in Extract D lie below the immigration figures for the whole of the period shown in the extract. [4 marks]

ⓔ Net migration equals immigration minus emigration. Although Extract D does not show explicitly the emigration figures for each of the years in the data, you can still work them out from the available data.

[07] Extract F (lines 1–3) states: 'Enlargement of the European Union has created a much larger internal market, which has led to both trade creation and trade diversion.' With the help of a diagram, explain how an internal market can create trade among the member countries of the European Union. [9 marks]

ⓔ The European Union has been enlarged on many occasions between when the UK, Ireland and Denmark joined the then 6 member states in 1973 and when Croatia joined the then 27 member states in 2013. The largest accession occurred in 2004 when ten countries, mostly in central Europe, joined the EU. Enlargement has, of course, created a bigger area of internal free trade within the Union.

[08] Do you agree that the benefits for the UK economy of migration from other EU countries into UK labour markets have exceeded the costs? Justify your answer. [25 marks]

ⓔ The [04] and [08] parts of a Context data-response question (and the second part of an essay question in Section B of the exam paper) often contain the words 'costs and benefits', 'advantages and disadvantages' or 'the case for versus the case against'. All three of these sets of words mean much the same thing: AQA is trying to help you to include both sides of the issue(s) posed by the question.

Student answer

[05] The percentage change is about 59%. I calculated this figure by placing the absolute growth in immigration (approximately 50,000) as a ratio of the figure in 2004 (approximately 85,000) and converting it into a percentage change.

ⓔ **1/2 marks awarded.** A sufficiently correct calculation to earn a mark, but the second mark has not been awarded because the student has ignored the instruction to present the calculation to two decimal places. Based on his figures, the answer should be 58.82%.

[06] Net migration is immigration minus emigration. Since we can assume that some UK citizens emigrated to other EU countries such as Spain in each of the years in the data period, this explains why the net migration figures lie below the immigration figures in each of the years.

ⓔ **4/4 marks awarded.** An accurate answer that does enough to earn all 4 marks.

[07] Enlargement means growing bigger. Enlargement of the EU has created a much larger internal market in which trade can take place. This has altered the pattern of trade between the now greater number of EU countries. For example, instead of importing sugar cane from countries outside the EU, as Britain did before it entered the EU in 1973, the high tariffs placed on, say, Jamaican sugar mean that the UK now either grows its own higher-cost sugar beet, or imports sugar beet from countries such as the Netherlands. A second example is German car manufacturers such as BMW building cars at lower cost in central European EU member states such as Hungary, rather than building them in higher-cost Munich in southern Germany. This creates trade within the EU.

ⓔ **3/9 marks awarded.** Unfortunately, this answer is weak. In the first place, the student has disobeyed the instruction to include a diagram. This instruction is generally present in a part [03] or [07] question. Mark schemes will advise examiners that 'if the response does not include a relevant diagram, the student cannot be awarded more than 5 marks'. In the second place, although the answer includes two examples of how the internal market has affected specialisation and trade, the answer lacks sufficient application of theory, for example the principle of comparative advantage.

[08] A labour market is a voluntary meeting of buyers and sellers of labour and can be illustrated by a diagram such as the one below.

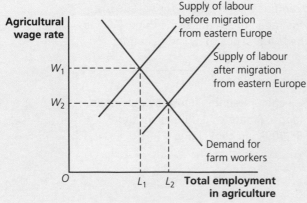

In my diagram, immigration from eastern Europe has shifted the supply curve of labour to the right in the labour market for farm workers. Before immigration, the farm wage rate was W_1. The shift to the right of the supply curve as immigrants flood the market leads to an excess supply of labour. More farm workers wish to work at wage rate W_1 than farmers wish to hire. The excess supply of labour causes the equilibrium wage rate to fall to a level that clears the market, namely W_2. Total employment has increased from L_1 to L_2, but this masks the fact that immigrants rather than British farm workers have the new jobs. There has been an increase in supply and an extension of demand.

As I have mentioned, migration of labour from other European Union countries takes jobs away from British workers. All governments have a duty to look after the interests of their own people, and this means protecting their jobs. Far stricter immigration controls should be imposed, and if it is necessary to do this, Britain should leave the European Union. It is a completely inefficient bureaucracy, ruling us from Brussels, and staffed by hundreds of thousands of eurocrats who we pay for. British taxes should be used to subsidise British workers, and not to pay the inflated salaries of unproductive foreign civil servants who want to do down the British economy. There is only a certain amount of jobs available, and we should have them and not Germans and Italians who we beat in the Second World War.

The only case, in my view, for allowing Polish workers into the UK is at least they are Europeans and not immigrants from Africa, who have little to offer to the UK economy and usually end up in prison. There are only costs involved when foreign workers come over here and steal our jobs. Immigrant workers drive down wages, thereby harming hard-working, decent British workers.

Nevertheless, many economists argue differently. As Extract F states, Polish migration has been a bit like 'adding the consumer demand of Liverpool to the economy in just two years'. Migration has stimulated aggregate demand in the UK economy. However, the main supposed benefits of inward migration may result from the supply-side effects of a larger skilled labour force. Before the recent period of inward migration into the UK of workers from other parts of the European Union, UK economic growth could seldom be sustained over a number of years. In those days, in the recovery and boom phases of the business cycle, the economy ran into the 'wall of inflation' as wage costs rose because of shortages of labour. From 2004 onwards, migrant workers arriving in the UK allowed the economy to grow without labour shortages emerging. As growth slowed down or a recession occurred, migrant workers returned to their countries of origin, without adding to the unemployment total in the UK. Migrant labour thus filled in gaps in the labour force.

ⓔ **12/25 marks awarded.** This is a rather strange answer. The first part of the answer contains some good analysis, though it is only indirectly related to the actual set question. However, the middle part of the answer is a classic rant that shows little evidence that the student has actually studied economics. It is worth warning students that questions on labour migration, together with questions on the European Union, tend to produce a disproportionate number of rants. (This is rather similar to political discussion in the UK in the lead-up in 2016 to the UK's referendum on continued EU membership!) As this question covers both these emotive topics, the temptation to rant has been magnified. This student has certainly worked up a head of steam. Whatever your political views, you need to keep them out of your answers. Engaging in a rant will do you no good in an economics exam. Pretend you are a neutral consultant being paid to give impartial advice to your clients. It is theoretically unsound to argue the 'lump of labour' theory, which assumes there is always a fixed number of jobs, and that workers from overseas inevitably take jobs from British workers.

In the final paragraph the student leaves behind the tendency to rant and writes some quite good economics. However, the answer would have benefited from drawing on some of the prompts in the extracts, for example overcrowding in private housing and cost pressures on English language training (on the debit side) and migrant workers as a source of tax revenue (on the benefit side).

On the basis of positive marking, we have placed this answer towards the bottom of Level 3 in the mark scheme (11–15 marks) as the answer just about meets the level descriptor of 'some reasonable analysis but generally unsupported evaluation'. (Positive marking means crediting what is good in the answer and not deducting marks for what is bad.) Additionally, the lack of a rounded conclusion means that more marks cannot be awarded.

ⓔ **Total score: 20/40 = Grade B/C border**

■ Essay questions

Note: The three essay questions that follow provide examples of questions typical of those set in Part B of Paper 1 in the A-level examination. Each of the questions is followed by a short guidance note. A student answer, along with examiner comments, follows on from the questions.

Essay 1 Behavioural economics

Total for this essay: 40 marks

[09] Explain the meaning of default choice with regard to people agreeing to donate organs such as livers and hearts in the event of their death. [15 marks]

[10] 'Governments which aim to solve problems such as the shortage of organs for transplant operations in hospitals are likely to be more successful if they follow the lessons learned from behavioural economics.'

With regard to the shortage of organs donated for transplant operations, discuss whether you agree or disagree with this statement. [25 marks]

ℯ These questions are testing your knowledge and understanding of one of the key concepts in the application of behavioural economics to government policy, namely the concept of default choice. Note that although the term 'default choice' is not mentioned in question [10], the information in question [09] indicates that you should centre the second part of your answer to [10] around the concept.

Student answer

[09] A default choice is an option that is selected automatically by the customers or clients of an organisation, unless an alternative is specified. In the case of organ donation, a default choice is set by a health care system such as the NHS to come into play in the tragic event that an individual is involved in a fatal accident. The default choice means that their vital organs can be transplanted to one or more other people in need of organs such as a liver or a kidney to save their lives.

There are two different default choices that can be set by policy makers when designing a choice architecture. (Choice architecture is a framework setting out different ways in which choices can be presented to consumers, and the impact of that presentation on consumer decision making.)

First, an opt-in system. This is when an individual has to explicitly agree to have their organs made available for transplantation in the event of their death. This default choice has traditionally been set in the UK. Individuals that have selected this choice carry organ donor cards in their wallets and purses and their details are kept on a national register.

The second default choice is an opt-out system. This is when an individual's organs are donated automatically in the event of a fatal accident unless the individual has explicitly opted out of the system.

In an opt-in system the assumption is that organs can only be donated if an individual has stated that they consent to this happening. In an opt-out system it is assumed that organs can only not be donated if an individual has objected.

e **12/15 marks awarded.** This is a good answer which reaches the mid-point of Level 3 (11–15 marks) in the mark scheme for the first part of an essay question. This requires a good response that is well organised and develops a selection of the key issues that are relevant to the question, shows sound knowledge and understanding of economic terminology, concepts and principles, with few, if any, errors, includes good application of relevant economic principles to the given context, where appropriate, and finally good use of data to support the response, and also includes well-focused analysis with clear, logical chains of reasoning. Depending on the nature of the question, not all these descriptors have to be met. With this question, it is difficult to see how a logical chain of reasoning can be included in an answer.

Student answer

[10] Governments are confronted with difficult policy decisions on a daily basis. Many of the economic decisions are based upon resource allocation. However, in the case of organ donation, policy makers have to decide if hospitals should run an opt-in or an opt-out system. The UK has traditionally run an opt-in system whereas Spain has operated an opt-out system, which has produced a greater supply of organs for transplant. As a result, policy makers in the UK have been under pressure to review their policy.

A shortage of organ donations means that patients have to wait for long periods of time for a suitable matching organ to become available. This is a major problem for two reasons. First, patients needing an organ transplant are sick, experience poor health and have a lower quality of life while they wait for a transplant. Second, the longer the wait, the higher the possibility a patient might die before a suitable match is found. Hence any policy that reduces the shortage of organ donors should be looked at carefully by government policy makers.

An opt-out system of organ donation will always create a larger supply of organs than an opt-in system. An opt-out system requires individuals to explicitly state that they do not want their organs used for transplantation in the event of a fatal accident whereas an opt-in system requires individuals to explicitly state that they do want their organs to be used in this manner. Given that a high number of the people who become organ donors are killed unexpectedly in unforeseeable circumstances, information problems exist.

The main information problem is that potential organ donors do not opt into an opt-in system because they do not expect to die. They will often be killed in tragic events, such as car accidents. In principle, they may consent to their organs being used for donation to save another person's life, but they do not opt into the system because they do not expect to die when they do.

However, by taking an individual's organs without explicit consent, the state is making two significant ethical assumptions. First, the individual would have opted out of the system had they had a major objection to their organs being used in this manner. There are many people, especially religious groups, who oppose organ donation on principle. By running an opt-out system, government policy makers are placing the emphasis on those opposed to organ donation to explicitly opt out. Second, the state is assuming that it has the right to take a person's organs without written consent and donate them to a stranger. Government policy makers might be operating with good intentions, but for libertarians an individual's rights must not be infringed upon by an over-powerful state.

The best way for the government to resolve this issue is to require all citizens to make a mandated choice. A mandated choice is a variation of a default choice which requires people to make a decision by law. This could be done when an individual applies for a driving licence, signs up to a GP practice, claims state benefits or files a tax return. A mandated choice system would mean that people who are happy for their organs to be transplanted after their death have explicitly given their consent, while individuals who are opposed can easily opt out of the system.

In conclusion, in facing this difficult issue, I believe that governments should operate an ethical organ donation system. A shortage of organs for donation may result in patients waiting for transplants suffering a lower quality of life, and in some cases death, but an unethical policy is unacceptable. An unethical market-based policy would be to pay desperate and low-income people to donate organs in exchange for financial payments to their families. Opt-in systems do lead to shortages of donations, but all of the donations made are gifts that an unfortunate individual has chosen to donate. An opt-out system will increase the number of donations made, but there is a chance that some organs will be donated against the will of the deceased individual. Therefore, the best policy would be for all citizens to have to make a mandated choice and for the health care system to keep an up-to-date register of people's choices.

e **21/25 marks awarded.** This is very good answer, which by displaying a depth and breadth of relevant knowledge reaches Level 5 (21–25 marks) in the mark scheme for the second part of an essay question. The grade descriptor for a Level 5 answer is sound, focused analysis and well-supported evaluation. Although the answer contains a conclusion, the conclusion lacks some conviction in terms of being fully supported by the content of the earlier part of the answer.

e **Total score: 33/40 = Grade A***

Essay 2 Price setting for a rock concert

Total for this essay: 40 marks

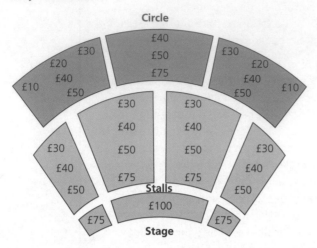

[11] The prices shown above are charged by an arena for tickets to see a rock concert. Explain why different prices are charged for tickets for events such as rock concerts.

[15 marks]

ⓔ This is a generally worded question that does not pin you down to considering only one possible explanation. For this question, it is wise to offer more than one explanation.

[12] Evaluate the economic reasons for and against charging the same price for every ticket at such events.

[25 marks]

ⓔ Following on from the advice note for question [11], there are several reasons for and against charging the same price for every ticket at an event if you have offered more than one explanation for different prices. Also note that for questions like this, the word 'such' in both parts of the question means that you don't have to support your answer with evidence drawn solely from rock concerts. You could, for example, consider the different prices charged to see a football match, or for a Wednesday afternoon theatre production versus a Saturday evening production.

Student answer

[11] The theory of price discrimination explains why different prices are charged for different tickets at events such as rock concerts. According to the question, prices ranging from a high of £100 to a low of £10 are charged by the arena for tickets to see the rock concert. However, to explain why different prices are charged, I shall pretend that there are only two different prices: £75 and £50. I shall also assume that 'diehard' fans of the rock group playing at the concert are prepared to pay £75, whereas 'ordinary' fans are only prepared to pay £50. This means that the two different groups of fans have different price elasticities of demand and different demand curves, which are shown on my diagram below.

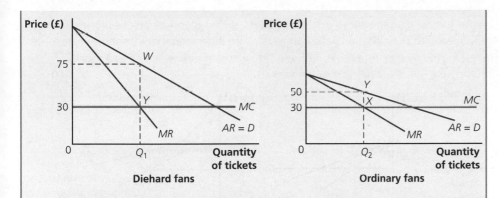

At all the prices that could be charged for seeing the rock concert, diehard demand is more inelastic than ordinary demand – indicating that the latter fans are less enthusiastic about the group performing at the rock concert. For both groups of fans, the downward-sloping demand curves in my diagram show average revenue (AR), but not marginal revenue (MR). In each case, the MR curve is twice as steep as the AR curve. The diagrams also assume (unrealistically) that the marginal cost (MC) of selling an extra ticket is always the same, namely £30. This explains the horizontal MC curve in both panels of the diagram.

To maximise profit, MR must equal MC in both sub-markets. As the diagrams show, this means that diehard fans pay the higher price of £75 for admission, with ordinary fans paying the lower entry price of £50. With the different prices being charged, Q_1 diehard fans and Q_2 ordinary fans watch the concert. The different prices charged result from the different price elasticities of demand. Profit is maximised when more price-sensitive ordinary fans pay less than the less price-sensitive diehard fans.

@ **12/15 marks awarded.** The student addresses the question with a focused explanation of how price discrimination leads to different prices being charged. The answer earns all the 10 marks available in the mark scheme for a single line of explanation together with 2 marks for a relevant diagram. In this case, the question does not ask for a diagram, but the mark scheme allows 2 marks for a relevant and accurate diagram, which is given in this answer. When a diagram is not mentioned in the question, full marks can be earned without a diagram, but for this question, full marks would require some mention of a second possible explanation of different prices being charged. For example, the student could have argued that the seats in an arena or concert hall are not homogeneous. For example, a seat in the front row of the stalls is a better 'product' with a better view of the stage than a seat at the end of the back row in the circle. Firms usually charge higher prices for better-quality products. Also, prices might vary according to the fame of the rock artists delivering the concert. Ticket prices for a Madonna concert are likely to be higher than for a little-known singer or band.

[12] The main reason in favour of charging the same price for tickets is that identical prices increase consumer surplus compared with the situation when there is price discrimination. Consumer surplus is the economic welfare enjoyed by consumers. I shall use the diagram below, which is a more sophisticated version of my earlier diagram, to explain why.

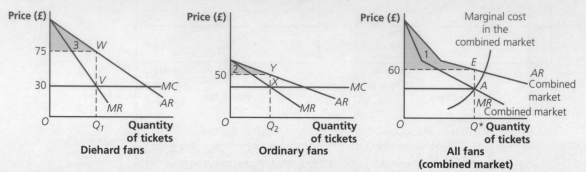

If different prices are charged to diehard and ordinary fans in my earlier example, firms increase profit by taking consumer surplus away from consumers and converting it into extra monopoly profit or above-normal profit. The left-hand and centre panels of the diagram are the same as the two panels in my earlier diagram, but I have added an extra panel to show the combined market (diehard and ordinary fans considered together). The combined market shows the average revenue curves added together, and likewise the marginal revenue curves.

If all fans pay the same price (£60), the consumer surplus they enjoy is shown by the shaded area (numbered 1) lying above £60 in the right-hand panel of the diagram. But if diehard fans are charged £75 a ticket while ordinary fans pay only £50, consumer surplus falls to equal the shaded areas numbered 3 and 2 in the left-hand and centre panels. (The shaded areas 3 and 2 are smaller than shaded area 1.) With price discrimination, the arena owner's profit has increased by transferring consumer surplus from consumers to the producer. Producer welfare (producer surplus) has increased at the expense of consumer welfare (consumer surplus). To prevent this form of possible consumer exploitation, all the rock fans at the concert should be charged the same price.

The main reason against charging the same price to all consumers is that it is not fair for the arena owner who takes the entrepreneurial risk in putting on the concert. If the promoter is prevented from charging different prices, it might not be worthwhile to put on the event, in which case fans who want to see the concert would suffer. Weighing up the different arguments, I think that price discrimination is justified, as both music lovers and the promoter of the event benefit.

ⓔ **18/25 marks awarded.** To emphasise once again, when answering the second part of an essay question (or the final part of a data-response question), to earn a high mark you have to evaluate as well as analyse. The analysis in this answer is accurate and well presented, and there is reasonable evaluation. Though the analysis is good, it does not extend beyond analysing the effect of identical prices and price discrimination on consumer surplus. Overall, the answer reaches the mid-point of Level 4 (16–20 marks) for which the descriptor is sound, focused analysis and some supported evaluation. Most of the answer focuses on a single benefit of charging the same price to all customers. The case against is cursory and a bit of an add-on. This lessens the scope for evaluation.

ⓔ **Total score: 30/40 = Grade A/A* border**

Essay 3 Monopoly and economic efficiency

Total for this essay: 40 marks

[13] 'Monopoly is statically inefficient but dynamically efficient.' Explain this
statement.

[15 marks]

(e) This question requires you to know the definitions of, and the differences
between, the main types of economic efficiency.

[14] Evaluate the view that the existence of monopoly can be justified, providing
the market is contestable.

[25 marks]

(e) In recent years, contestable market theory has had a major impact on UK
monopoly policy. The theory implies that, provided there is adequate potential for
competition, a conventional regulatory policy is superfluous.

Student answer

[13] A firm is statically efficient only when it produces at the lowest point on its
average total cost (ATC) curve. Points of static efficiency are shown at A
and B on the two short-run average cost ($SRATC$) curves in my diagram.

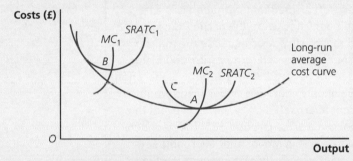

Dynamic efficiency, by contrast, results from improvements in static
efficiency that take place over time. The development of a new process for
manufacturing a good, which reduces average costs of production, is an
example of dynamic efficiency. In my diagram, the movement from $SRATC_1$
to $SRATC_2$ represents an improvement in dynamic efficiency, resulting
from the firm's ability to benefit from economies of scale, which enables
the firm to move to a lower short-run average cost curve.

Providing the market is large enough, a monopoly can benefit from
economies of scale. It can produce on $SRATC_2$, whereas smaller
competitive firms might be constrained to producing on $SRATC_1$. A
monopoly is thus likely to be dynamically efficient. It could also be
statically efficient on $SRATC_2$, but only if it produces at point A on this
curve. However, because monopolies often restrict output in order
to raise the price they can charge and make above-normal profit, the
monopoly may in fact end up producing at point C. This point is statically
inefficient. My analysis has shown, therefore, that a monopoly can be
dynamically efficient but statically inefficient.

e **11/15 marks awarded.** This is a good answer, but it does not go quite far enough. With one exception, what the student has written is relevant and accurate. However, the answer defines static efficiency solely in terms of productive efficiency. She needs to explain that monopoly is allocatively inefficient ($P > MC$).

---

[14] Compared with perfect competition, a monopoly has the incentive to innovate (because the firm can enjoy the fruits of successful innovation in the form of monopoly profit), and by growing, it can achieve economies of scale and reduce costs.

In recent years, the theory of contestable markets has also been used to justify monopoly. A market is contestable when a new firm can enter the market without being deterred by entry barriers, and without incurring sunk costs that are irrecoverable, should the firm decide to leave the market.

To develop my answer further, I shall use the federal court case in America, in which the US Justice Department prosecuted Microsoft, with a view to getting the court to break up Microsoft into a number of smaller firms, so as to reduce its alleged monopoly position in the PC software market. Economists hired by Microsoft argued that, although it is a monopoly in the sense that the company has over 90% of the PC operating system market, Microsoft has no monopoly power because the market is contestable. They argued: (i) if Microsoft acted as a profit-maximising monopolist, it would charge a price of over $100 for its Windows operating system; (ii) because of an absence of entry barriers, other firms would then enter the market and undercut Microsoft's price; (iii) to prevent this happening, Microsoft actually charges a price (around $35) that is much lower than the profit-maximising price. This means that Microsoft sets limit prices for its products. Microsoft argues that consumers benefit from its limit-pricing policy. Conversely, consumers would suffer greatly (from higher prices and less technical innovation and new products) if the US courts ever decided to force Microsoft to split into smaller firms.

My conclusion is, if a monopoly behaves 'virtuously' and does not abuse its monopoly power, and if the market is sufficiently contestable, its dominant position can be justified – but only as long as the firm continues to behave itself. To try to ensure this outcome, the monopoly must be policed by a regulatory agency set up by the government. Even then, however, there is always the danger that the agency, lacking sufficient technical knowledge of the firm(s) it is regulating, will be ineffective and/ or subject to regulatory capture.

---

e **20/25 marks awarded.** This is an excellent answer, which displays a depth and breadth of relevant knowledge. Although the answer contains a good conclusion, rather more is needed on contestable markets to reach Level 5. We have placed the answer at the top of Level 4 (16–20 marks).

e **Total score: 31/40 = Grade A/A* border**

■Investigation question

Note: The investigation question that follows provides an example of questions typical of those set in Part B of Paper 3 in the A-level examination. A student answer, along with examiner comments, follows on from the questions.

Source booklet: Freshwater flooding in the UK

Extract A: Possible causes of freshwater flooding

Extract B: Risk of floods in England up due to cuts in government funding, says the National Audit Office

Extract C: Flooding in the UK: selected key statistics

Extract D: UK building 10,000 homes a year on floodplains

Extract A Possible causes of freshwater flooding

Freshwater flooding must not be confused with coastal flooding. The latter is caused by high tides and by storm surges pushing towards land from the sea. Freshwater flooding, by contrast, is caused by inland rainfall falling on hills and then making 5 its way downhill eventually to reach the coast. The two forms of flooding can of course be linked, most usually when rainwater flowing down a river basin meets a tidal sea surge pushing up the river's estuary. 10

The first cause of freshwater flooding is of course heavy rainfall (or snow melt). Many experts now agree that this is the result of acceleration in the process of global warming. The question arises as to whether the adverse effects of freshwater 15 flooding result from market failure, government failure, the response of insurance companies, or decisions made by the victims themselves.

The second cause of freshwater flooding is the way that land and rivers respond to this 20 deluge. If land and rivers are managed to enable them to hold back the water, slow the flow to the lowlands (where almost everyone lives) and reduce the height of the flood peak, flood defences at the bottom of the catchment are 25 less likely to be overwhelmed. If, instead, the water runs quickly off the land and rushes down the rivers as quickly as possible, the chances of disaster downstream are significantly raised.

Reducing the likelihood of devastating floods 30 means considering a river's catchment as a whole, rather than treating different sections of it as isolated components. It means retaining water in the hills (where most of the rain falls) for as long as possible, by allowing trees to grow 35 and bogs to form.

In 2016, George Monbiot, an environmentalist, accused the government's Environment Secretary, Elizabeth Truss, of kowtowing to the interests of the farming lobby by adopting 40 exactly the wrong and opposite policy towards rainfall runoff. At the Oxford farming conference on Wednesday 6 January 2016, Monbiot said that Truss revealed she intends to go ahead with her long-standing plan to allow farmers 45 to dredge and clear the water courses passing through their land, without oversight, regulation or consideration of the impacts downstream, in order to prevent their fields from flooding.

Source: various news sources, 2015 and 2016

Extract B Risk of floods in England up due to cuts in government funding, says the National Audit Office

Flood defence spending fell by 10% over the course of the coalition government, leaving half of the country's defences with 'minimal' maintenance, says a National Audit Office report. The cuts are a false economy. 5

Five million homes in England are at risk of flooding and the government's own assessment shows climate change is increasing the risk by driving more extreme weather. The NAO report said every £1 spent on flood defences prevented almost £10 in damage. The report noted: 'Ad-hoc emergency spending is less good value than sustained maintenance.' 10

Margaret Hodge MP, chair of parliament's Public Accounts Committee, said: 'I am deeply concerned that current levels of spending are not enough to maintain flood protection.' She said the cuts by the Department for Environment, Food and Rural Affairs (Defra) were 'alarming'. 15

In reply, flooding minister Dan Rogerson said the NAO, which scrutinises public spending on behalf of parliament, had used the wrong numbers. 'The NAO has drawn conclusions on funding based on inappropriate comparisons.' 20

'Cameron promised that "money was no object" when it came to flooding, but the NAO report makes it clear that spending on flood defences is down,' said Maria Eagle, Shadow Environment Secretary. 'Ignoring the evidence on climate change has led to the government making the 25 30

wrong choices.' She said a Labour government would 'reprioritise' long-term spending to cut flood risk.

'The NAO report highlights the need for proper flood risk management and the need to invest in it now,' said Paul Cobbing, chief executive of the National Flood Forum, which represents and supports community groups. 'We have to rise to the challenge because clearly what we are doing at the moment is not creating safer communities.' 35 40

MPs warned the government in June 2014 that devastating winter floods could hit England again unless cuts to flood defence budgets were reversed. Money for the maintenance of rivers and flood defences was at the 'bare minimum', they said. 45

Flood-stricken communities have been left without planned defences following government funding cuts. In 2012, 294 flood defence schemes across England had been left unbuilt due to budget cuts. A Friends of the Earth spokesman said: 'The NAO's findings are a damning indictment of government neglect. The government is letting flood defences crumble as sea levels rise and extreme weather worsens.' He said the government must plug the £500 million hole in flood defence spending identified by its official advisers, the Committee on Climate Change. 50 55 60

Source: various news reports, November 2014

Extract C Flooding in the UK: selected key statistics

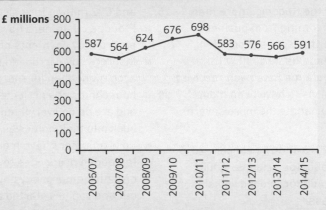

DEFRA funding for flood defences in real terms (2012/13 prices)

Source: DEFRA

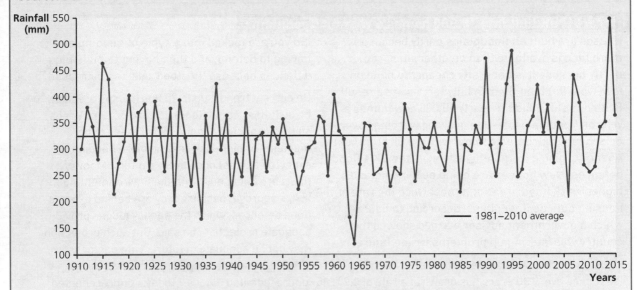

Rainfall, England, 1910–2015

Source: Met Office

Following the devastating floods caused by storms Desmond, Eva and Frank during December 2015 and over the New Year in 2016, insurers are today releasing new figures to demonstrate the scale of the response by the sector. 5

Statistics collected by the Association of British Insurers (ABI) show more than 3,000 families are now in alternative accommodation while repairs are made to their homes. The average expected payout for each domestic flood claim is £50,000 10 – compared with an average from the 2013/2014 winter storms of £31,000.

£24 million of emergency payments have been made to both families and businesses to spend on immediate needs, for example food, clothing and 15 staff salaries. Costs for alternative home or business accommodation are paid directly by insurers.

The latest estimates suggest the final amount ABI members will spend on customers affected by flood damage is likely to be around £1.3 billion. 20

■ Of the £24 million emergency payments made so far, £9 million has been to domestic customers and £15 million to businesses.

- Customers have made nearly 15,000 claims for property damaged by the flooding, more than 5,000 of these claims coming from business customers. There are thousands of smaller claims for storm damage being dealt with. 25
- A total of 5,600 motor claims have been received.
- More than 8,300 initial visits have been made by loss adjusters, who handle the more severe claims. 30

Between 23 December 2013 and 28 February 2016:
- Insurers received 17,500 flood claims: 9,000 from homeowners, 5,400 for flooded vehicles and 3,100 from businesses. 35
- Of the £446 million of claims, an estimated £276 million is expected to be paid to flooded homeowners, £149 million to business owners and £22 million to vehicle owners. 40
- Flooded customers have already received emergency payments of £27 million.
- Insurers have arranged temporary alternative accommodation for more than 2,100 flooded households at a projected cost of £24 million, 45 and are doing everything possible to get people back into their homes as soon as it is safe to do so.
- Loss adjusters have made over 6,500 visits to flooded properties to assess the damage, organise emergency payments, and get drying 50 out and repairs started as quickly as possible.

Source: Association of British Insurers (ABI)

Extract D UK building 10,000 homes a year on floodplains

Houses are built on floodplains partly because more land is available than on other sites, and partly because it is generally cheaper to build on low-lying flat land than on hilly terrain. As a result, Britain is still building nearly 10,000 new homes a 5 year on floodplains despite growing warnings over episodes of extreme flooding, with the Environment Agency urging a 'complete rethink' of the UK's flood defences. New houses are being built in England's highest-risk flood areas at almost twice the rate of 10 housing outside floodplains, according to figures which a government adviser warned showed the country was 'storing up problems for the future'.

Housing stock in areas where flooding is likely at least once every 30 years has grown at a rate of 1.2% 15 per year since 2011, according to analysis by the Committee on Climate Change (CCC). By contrast, housing outside of floodplains – in areas with less than a 1-in-1,000-year chance of flooding – increased by an average 0.7% a year over the same period. 20

Lord Krebs, head of the CCC's adaptation sub-committee, said: 'We are building faster in the floodplain than anywhere else.

'If the planning system is going to allow people to carry on building in the floodplain, we have to be 25 aware we are storing up problems for the future because flooding is going to get more frequent.

'So you are locked into a cycle of building and having to defend, and then having to build bigger defences because the flood risk has increased.' 30

On current trends, up to 20,000 houses are likely to be built this year in flood-risk areas. Lord Krebs said he expected about 4,500 of these to be medium- or high-risk areas, where flooding is expected at least once every century. Many of 35 these are being built with the Environment Agency (EA)'s approval because they are behind existing flood defences, which the agency judges provide adequate protection, he said. But such protection may not be adequate in future, with defences 40 already being overtopped in recent weeks by 'unprecedented' floods. 'Today's unprecedented may be tomorrow's norm,' he warned. Thousands of other homes in at-risk areas may be being built without the EA's oversight because they are in small 45 developments of less than ten houses, he said.

Lord Krebs warned the continued spread of concrete and paving tiles over gardens and other green spaces was worsening the risk of flooding because it prevented water draining. 50

Farmers and grouse shooting estates had also increased the risk for urban areas by draining peat bogs on surrounding uplands, which used to provide a natural 'sponge' for rainfall.

Source: various news reports

Section B

Answer all questions in this section.

Refer to source booklet for Extracts A, B, C and D.

Total for this investigation: 50 marks

Freshwater flooding in the UK

Investigation

Scenario

You are an economist reporting to a recently formed lobby group, Noah s Ark, which represents small businesses and householders who have been badly affected by freshwater flooding. Noah's Ark has requested that you provide answers to three key questions.

Referring to the source booklet, study Extracts A, B and C and then use these and your own economic knowledge to help you answer questions 31 and 32. There is an additional news report, Extract D, which is to be used with the other extracts to help answer question 33.

31 To what extent, if at all, do the data support the view that the growing threat of freshwater flooding results from inadequate government investment in flood defences? You must use the data in Extract C to support your assessment. [10 marks]

Student answer

[31] The data in Extract C provide clear evidence that the British government has cut investment spending on flood defence and that the average rainfall in England has significantly increased since 2010.

According to the data shown from Defra, spending on flood defence was cut from £698 million in 2010/11 to £583 million in 2011/12. Government spending had risen to £591 million in 2014/15 but even then spending in real terms was cut by 15.3% between 2010/11 and 2014/15.

The second chart shown in Extract C shows rainfall in England between 1910 and 2015. In the period shown the average rainfall was 325 mm. However, since 2012 the rainfall in England has been higher than this average. In 2014 England saw the highest rainfall, with 550 mm, which is the highest recorded over the entire period.

The data provides support for the claim that cuts in government investment to flood defences have resulted in a growing threat of freshwater flooding, but further evidence is needed to back up this argument.

The National Audit Office report cited in Extract B is very clear that the cuts introduced by the government are responsible for the increasing freshwater flooding. According to the National Audit Office, 'every £1 spent on flood defences prevented almost £10 in damage' (Extract B). Given that between 2010/11 and 2011/12 spending on flood defences was cut by £115 million, it is fair to conclude that government cuts resulted in over

£1 billion worth of unnecessary flood damage. This figure is supported by the evidence in Extract C from the Association of British Insurers, which estimated that damaged caused by the 2015–2016 floods will cost £1.3 billion. It is also logical to conclude that if investment spending was cut, measures were not taken to build stronger defences and prepare local communities for surges of floodwater. Therefore, when heavy rain did occur, the defences in place were inadequate.

However, the government minister quoted in Extract B, Dan Rogerson, claimed that the numbers used by the NAO were wrong and that the conclusions were drawn 'on funding based on inappropriate comparisons'. It is difficult to develop this argument because the extract does not provide any further explanation. None of the other extracts supports this statement.

(e) **10/10 marks awarded.** An excellent answer, which does exactly what is required by the wording of the question, namely to discuss to what extent, if at all, the data support the view that the growing threat of freshwater flooding results from inadequate government investment in flood defences. The student makes good use of the data in Extract C.

32 Lines 14–18 of Extract A state: 'The question arises as to whether the adverse effects of freshwater flooding result from market failure, government failure, the response of insurance companies, or decisions made by the victims themselves.' Explain how 'decisions made by the victims themselves' may contribute to the adverse effects of freshwater flooding.   [15 marks]

[32] There are two main ways in which the victims of freshwater flooding may have contributed to flooding. The first is that landowners have not taken preventative action to protect their land. As the Environmental Secretary quoted in Extract A makes clear, one of the reasons why farmland has flooded in the past is because farmers did not 'dredge and clear the water courses passing through their land'.

When a farmer's land is flooded, significant damage is caused. If crop harvests are lost and/or repair bills run into thousands of pounds, the average costs of farming will rise. The ABI estimated in Extract C that 5,000 claims for property damaged by flooding came from businesses and between 2013 and 2016 £149 million was estimated to be claimed by business owners. Farmers will make up a significant proportion of these claims, therefore it is reasonable to conclude that had they taken action to protect their land, they could have avoided the damage. As can be seen in the diagram below, as flooding takes place the supply curve of farm produce shifts to the left. This is because farmers incur significant costs when their businesses are hit by floods, which damages their crop yields and pushes prices up for consumers.

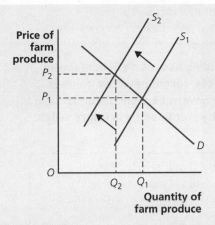

The second way in which victims may have adversely contributed to the effect of flooding is by themselves contributing to global warming. The experts cited in Extract A say that the increase in flooding has occurred as a 'result of the acceleration in the process of global warming'. If UK households have been contributing to the process of global warming over many years by dumping negative externalities into the atmosphere, say through driving their cars, they have made the likelihood of heavy rain and severe storms more probable.

Climate change has been accelerated by CO_2 emissions being dumped into the atmosphere. This has taken place in the UK as firms and households have burned fossil fuels to generate energy. However, the price they have paid for energy (equal to C_1 in the diagram) has been lower than the social cost (equal to C_2 in the diagram) because the market price has not reflected the cost of the negative externality. As can be seen in the diagram, the social cost is higher than the market price. By imposing a carbon tax, the government may be able to reduce consumption to the socially optimal level at Q_2, at which the marginal social cost of production is shown at C_3.

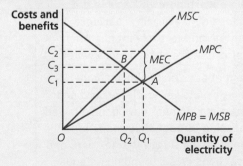

In a free market, the price is too low and too much of the product (Q_1) has been demanded. This has resulted in significant quantities of CO_2 emissions being dumped into the atmosphere and speeding up the process of climate change. This is leading to more extreme weather conditions and heavier rainfall. As the rainfall chart in Extract C shows, 2014 saw 70 mm more rainfall than any year since 1995.

🅔 **13/15 marks awarded.** Once again, an excellent and focused answer, which earns high marks. However, there is some confusion about externalities – are they production externalities or consumption externalities?

33 Taking into account the information about building houses on floodplains in Extract D, and the other evidence in the extracts, recommend two courses of action that either people themselves or the government should undertake in order to reduce the adverse effects of freshwater flooding in future years. Justify your recommendations.

[25 marks]

---

[33] In order to reduce the likelihood of freshwater flooding in the future the British government needs to take a lead and set out a clear policy direction. There is a strong body of evidence that suggests that freshwater flooding will be a very real danger in the future due to heavy rainfall or snow melt. As Extract A states: 'Many experts now agree that this is the result of acceleration in the process of global warming.' The causes of global warming can be tackled by the British government, therefore it has to introduce policies that enable the UK to cope best with the dangers. There are two main courses of action that the government should pursue: a policy that seeks to prevent freshwater flooding by holding back water on higher ground for as long as possible, and a housing policy that manages where and how housing is built in floodplains.

The government needs to develop a policy that holds back water on higher ground for as long as possible following heavy rain. The purpose of the policy would be to keep water at a higher level for as long as possible to stop the flood defences at a lower level from being overwhelmed. As Extract A says, if 'the water runs quickly off the land and rushes down the rivers as quickly as possible, the chances of disaster downstream are significantly raised'.

There are three main ways in which the government needs to develop a course of action. First, it needs to encourage the growing of more trees on higher ground. Trees can absorb significant quantities of water, so by planting more trees on higher ground the government will enable the land to absorb more water following periods of heavy rain. Therefore, the government should introduce a tree-planting and forestry management programme to cultivate forests on higher ground to absorb more water.

Second, the government needs to ensure that bogs and fields on higher ground retain more water to prevent flooding on lower levels. According to Extract A, this has not been happening because farmers have been allowed to 'dredge and clear the water courses passing through their land…in order to prevent their fields from flooding'. Extract D says that farmers and grouse shooting estates have drained 'peat bogs on surrounding uplands, which used to provide a natural "sponge" for rainfall'. The farmers and grouse estates have clearly pursued this course of action for commercial reasons, but the consequence has been to increase the risk of flooding for those living in urban areas on lower ground. Thus, the government should introduce a system of subsidies for farmers and grouse estates to encourage them to maintain bogs in strategic areas and allow designated fields to flood when necessary. The cost of these subsidies will not be cheap, but if they prevent significant flood damage which runs into billions of pounds they will be worth it.

Third, the government should consider how to best prepare low-lying land for increased heavy rain. Lord Krebs warned in Extract D that the increased spread of concrete and paving tiles over gardens and green space is preventing draining and increasing the risk of flooding. This has been an undesirable side effect of the decision of many households across the UK to undertake home improvements, such as driveways in their front gardens and decking in the back. At a national level, government could introduce a policy which aims to encourage households to plant more trees and shrubs in their gardens. At a local level, councils could plant more trees in open spaces along streets and on commons. Individually these actions would have little impact, but if aggregated across the nation the results would be significant.

The second main course of action the government should consider is managing housebuilding on floodplains. The UK has a highly inelastic housing supply and a highly inelastic demand for housing. In the last five years, house prices in the UK have increased significantly. As a result, there has been a tremendous temptation for houses to be built on land that is on a floodplain. According to Extract D, 'Britain is building nearly 10,000 new homes a year on floodplains despite growing warnings over episodes of extreme flooding'. In recent years, flood damage has caused significant damage to UK households and businesses. Extract C states that between 23 December 2013 and 28 February 2016 'insurers received 17,500 flood claims: 9,000 from homeowners, 5,400 for flooded vehicles, and 3,100 from businesses'. With heavy rain and severe storms expected to become more common in the future, the government needs to consider its housing policy management carefully. The government should consider a twofold course of action.

First, the government needs to tighten planning controls. It is poor public policy for the government to allow housebuilding to take place on property that it knows has a high probability to flood. However, in Extract D Lord Krebs says that at present '20,000 houses are likely to be built this year in flood-risk areas'. Therefore the government needs to introduce new legislation preventing construction firms from building in high-risk areas.

Second, the government needs to build stronger flood defences in some areas to protect low-level housing. It is significantly cheaper to build housing on low-level than on high-level land. The UK has a housing shortage and needs to build more homes to meet existing and future demand. Hence it is inevitable that houses will be built on floodplains. However, this has to be planned and managed by the government to make sure that construction only takes place in designated areas where the government has assessed the risks and built up necessary defences. This will require a coordinated government policy and considerable investment in flood defences.

Ultimately the government needs to take a leading role in helping to prevent future flood damage. Climate change is happening and whatever the causes will mean that heavy rainfall and severe storms are going to hit Britain on a regular basis in coming years. In order to deal with this challenge, the government needs to play an active role managing the situation. It needs to plan for the future and coordinate economic activity. This can be achieved through policies that seek to create incentives for farmers and grouse estates to manage the land better and absorb high-level water in periods of heavy rain. Incentives can also be created for building firms to ensure that new homes are built in areas protected by flood defences. The government must also play a direct role in planting trees in specific areas to absorb water and tightening planning controls to prevent building in high-risk areas. If the government follows these recommendations, it will help avoid costly flood damage in the future.

e 11/25 marks awarded. Though the answer contains a lot of relevant information and draws well on the extracts, including Extract D, it contains a number of significant flaws. In the first place, by ranging over a number of possible policy actions, the answer disobeys the instruction in the question to 'recommend two courses of action'. Second, by considering too many possible courses of action, the answer ends up being thin on evaluation. Displaying this skill is necessary in an answer to the last part of an investigation question to reach the highest Level 5 (21–25 marks), which requires 'supported evaluation throughout the response and a well-supported final recommendation'. Third, there are a fair number of unsubstantiated assertions, for example that there is a highly inelastic demand for housing. We have placed this answer at the bottom of Level 3 (11–15 marks), for which the level descriptor is 'some reasonable analysis but generally unsupported evaluation'.

e Total score: 34/50 = Grade A/B border

Individual economic decision making

1 Total utility is the total satisfaction or fulfilment of need derived from the total quantity of a good or service consumed. Marginal utility is the additional satisfaction or fulfilment of need yielded by the last unit consumed of a good or service.

2 Asymmetric information is a situation in which one party in a transaction has more or superior information compared with another. Symmetric information is when the same information is available to all parties in the transaction.

3 An example of irrational behaviour is someone knowingly behaving in a way that is against their self-interest, for example walking on a rainy night on the edge of the pavement and thus increasing the likelihood of being splashed by a passing car.

4 Thinking fast would be shooting on sight as soon as a pass is received. Thinking slow would be when taking a penalty, deciding not to shoot until the goalkeeper has shown the direction in which he is going to dive.

Production, costs and revenue

5 Diminishing marginal returns occur in the short run when at least one factor of production is fixed. Decreasing returns to scale occur in the long run when all factors of production are variable.

6 The rent paid for the lease of business premises is a fixed cost, as is the annual business rate paid to government. The hourly wage rate paid to casual labour is a variable cost, as is the electricity bill paid for the use of electricity for heating and lighting.

7 Both the *AVC* and the *ATC* fall, when *MC* is below the curves. As soon as *MC* rises above the curves, the curves start to rise. Both the *AVC* and the *ATC* curves are thus U-shaped.

8 A rise in wage costs causes a firm's costs of production to increase, and as labour becomes relatively more expensive than capital, firms are likely to employ less labour and more capital, adopting more capital-intensive methods of production.

9 Marginal revenue is the extra sales revenue a firm receives from selling one more unit of a good or service. Marginal returns are the extra output that an extra worker contributes to total output.

Perfect competition, imperfectly competitive markets and monopoly

10 Agricultural markets, stock markets and foreign exchange markets may approximate to perfect competition.

11 Because no real-world market displays simultaneously all the six conditions of perfect competition.

12 Monopoly is one firm only in a market. Monopoly power is the power to restrict output, to raise prices and to restrict consumer choice. All imperfectly competitive firms, as well as monopolies, possess this power to a greater or lesser extent.

13 The concentration ratio for a pure monopoly is 100 or 100%.

14 Competitive oligopolists may be adversely affected by uncertainty as to how rival firms will react to their price and output decisions. They may decide to collude to reduce or eliminate this uncertainty. Such collusion may enable the participating firms to make larger monopoly profits.

15 According to the kinked demand theory of oligopoly, a competitive oligopolist faces two perceived demand curves for its product, the first with respect to raising its selling price and the second with respect to cutting its selling price. The kink occurs at the junction of the two demand curves, with the first curve being relatively price elastic and the second curve being relatively price inelastic.

16 No; differences can also be explained by differences in costs of production.

17 Economic welfare is the happiness, utility, satisfaction, pleasure and fulfilment of need received by economic agents. Consumer surplus is a measure of consumer welfare, while producer surplus is a measure of producer welfare.

18 Monopoly may lead to market failure as a result of monopolies restricting output, raising the prices they charge, restricting consumer choice and exercising their producer sovereignty.

The labour market

19 Composite demand is demand for a good which has more than one use: for example, barley can be used as an animal feed or to make beer. This example also illustrates derived demand, since the demand for barley is derived from the demand for meat products and the demand for beer. The demand for labour is also a derived demand, which increases when the demand for the goods workers help to produce goes up.

20 If workers attempt to sell their labour at a wage rate above the ruling market wage existent in a perfectly competitive labour market, they will price themselves out of jobs. To remain employed in such a market, workers must passively accept the ruling market wage determined by market forces in the labour market as a whole.

21 Unlike employers in a perfectly competitive labour market who are passive price-takers, a monopsony employer has the power to force down the wage rate paid to workers. Possessing this power, the monopsonist is a price-maker, the wage rate being the price of labour.

22 In 2016, the national minimum wage is the minimum pay per hour that workers are entitled to by law, while the national living wage is a voluntary rate that employers can choose to commit to paying. A new legally binding 'national living wage' of £7.20 per hour is being introduced in April 2017 for all working people aged 25 and over.

The distribution of income and wealth: poverty and inequality

23 Income is a continuous flow or stream of payments, whereas wealth is a historical accumulation that has built up over time. Wealth is measured as a 'snapshot' at a particular point in time, whereas income is measured over a particular time period, for example hourly, weekly, monthly, quarterly or annually.

24 A tax is progressive if the tax paid rises at a faster rate than income. It is regressive if the tax paid rises at a slower rate than income. It is proportionate if the tax paid rises at exactly the same rate as income.

The market mechanism, market failure and government intervention in markets

25 A public good such as national defence is defined by its characteristics of non-excludability, non-rivalry and non-rejectability. A merit good such as health care is defined, first in terms of the positive externalities generated when it is consumed, and second by the likelihood that the long-term private benefits of consumption exceed the short-term private benefits of consumption.

26 Productive efficiency occurs when average costs of production are minimised and when it is impossible to increase production of one good without reducing production of at least one other good. Allocative efficiency occurs when the price charged for a good or service equals the marginal cost of producing the good ($P = MC$), or more strictly when the price equals the marginal social cost of producing the good ($P = MSC$).

27 Privatisation is the transfer of assets, for example firms and industries, from public ownership to private ownership. Deregulation is the removal of previously imposed regulations. Privatisation and deregulation, which can be regarded as complementary policies in a wider policy of economic liberalisation, are favoured by supply-side economists (see Student Guide 4).

Note: **Bold** page numbers indicate key term definitions.

Index

Index